ADVAN

What if the unthinkable happened? Wait... If it is unthinkable, why do we think about it? If we can think about it, we can talk about it—and in talking about it we gain power over it. Lark Dean Galley courageously shares her story about her son's death by suicide in a way that is not only clear and authentic, but powered with psychologically healing principles. *Learning To Breathe Again* opens up a necessary conversation in a way that saves lives and heals hearts.

– PAUL H. JENKINS, PhD, PSYCHOLOGIST
Author of *Pathological Positivity* and founder of
Live On Purpose Central; drpauljenkins.com

Lark Galley has turned a courageous eye to her difficult childhood to examine her father's mental illness and its impact on her life and family. With thoughtful reflection, she lives her son Christian's life and his death by suicide—her own struggles, growth and forgiveness. This story will resonate with many bereaved parents. It is Lark's gift of love to Christian and to you.

– KATHIE SUPIANO, PhD, LCSW, F-GSA, FT, APHSW-C
Associate Professor and Director,
Caring Connections: A Hope and Comfort in Grief Program
University of Utah College of Nursing

As a mother who has also lost her adult son to suicide, I was very touched by Lark's book. Although our life experiences are different, our feelings about this kind of loss and how much more connected we are now to our sons are similar. It is our faith and this new heavenly connection that keeps us moving forward in our mission to enlighten and educate people about the truths about suicide. Thank you, Lark, for putting into words the hard things we want to express.

— CAREY CONLEY

Speaker and Co-Author of *Keep Looking Up: Transforming Grief into Hope After Tragedy* (co-author is my daughter, Laurel Conley Wilson)

As a parent, Lark's book gave me much to think about. She doesn't sugar coat their relationships, and her brutal honesty and vulnerability help the reader understand the heart of the family members. I have a son who is just five months older than Christian. Lark's hard-won insights hit home and helped me come to needed realizations. I'm asking my husband to read the book, as well. I genuinely believe Christian's story and his parents' honest struggles will improve relationships and save lives.

— JODI ORGILL BROWN

Author of *The Sun Still Shines: How a Brain Tumor Helped Me See the Light*

This is a brave, honest story. In her book, Lark beautifully illustrates that relationships are everything, and there is always hope to be had.

— JULIE LEE

Author of *I See You*; www.julieleespeaks.com

Lark and I were immediate friends. She is driven, clear and honest—all qualities I admire in others. We even vacationed together and got the joy of knowing each other's children. There are inside jokes inspired by Christian and his full-of-fun approach to life. When Christian died, we were stunned. We talked to our children, who once again were impacted by death. Their baby sister had died years earlier due to a rare genetic issue. Immediately, I offered my friend what another friend had done for me in the wake of our loss—weekly lunches. Lark, being the driven woman she is, didn't have time for that! She had a mission! We now have another joke inspired by Christian: Lark not having time for lunches and my wanting to talk about all the gushy feelings.

When I heard she was writing a book, I thought, 'This will be a clinical approach to death by suicide—the facts, figures, etc.' I was wrong. I had deeply underestimated my friend. Yes, the book goes into the epidemic that we all face. It offers solutions, resources, and how to prevent it, just as I thought Lark would; she is solutions based. Even more, she goes into her life, her strengths, and her weaknesses. She doesn't glorify or excuse herself. She hands you her beating heart, hers and her son's. As an author myself, I know it is not an easy thing to be that vulnerable without having a pity party on the page. I highly recommend you read this book with your spouse and discuss the ideas and topics of the book with your children. You will find the book drives home the lessons of forgiveness, purpose, conversation, and parenting in a clear voice without ego of the author, but rather an honest loving account of the value of each human soul.

– LETA GREENE

Author of *How to Embrace Your Inner Hotness*,
Love, Me Too, and coming title *More Laughter Than Tears*

When making your way through grief and pain, a guide who has walked a similar path is a tremendous blessing. Often helping to avoid missteps and shorten this painful path. Lark Dean Galley shares her powerful, personal and heart wrenching story for the benefit of others. Lark is one of the strongest women I know. Her strength comes from knowing when she needed to change direction in her life, step into this space and devote her life to this cause. If life has taken you into a place of grief and pain, you need to read this book. It will help your heart heal.

– JON GOSSETT
Founder, Life's Worth Living Foundation

When I saw the news about Lark's son, I could not imagine what she was feeling at the time. I went to high school with Lark and saw her take charge of her family and ration food to her siblings. I did not know the extreme craziness of the situation until I read her manuscript.

I, too, have experienced the loss of loved ones, and I shared my experience in my book on grief. My book is about three people I was close to who died. The grief built up over time until I could not get out of bed. I was debilitated. I was forced to deal with my grief because in the past I had swept it under the rug.

There are no words to describe the intense loneliness felt after the death of a loved one—the mixture of sadness and relief that your loved ones are in a better place. I now know what I believe happens after death. The knowledge has made the passing of people emotionally easier for me.

I reached out to Lark in the hope my book and experiences would somehow help her with her loss and encourage her to author her book. Writing helps a person heal and allows others to heal. Her book is phenomenal and is a vulnerable, open story of her life. She talks openly about her relationship with her son, her childhood, and many more lessons in life.

If you are looking for a book to help you get beyond grief, especially after the loss of a dear loved one, this book will enlighten and feed your soul.

– LINDA RAWSON

Author of *Reflections on Grief: Loss, Love, and Happiness*

———————————

This was an extremely powerful message regarding the life and journey of Lark and her son, Christian. I appreciated the experiences Lark shares from her childhood and family dynamics that she references to bring perspective to her story. Her courage to be vulnerable with her relationship as a mother to her children, especially Christian, was and is a true testimony to her commitment to mental health awareness and suicide prevention. I recommend this book to all parents who have experienced the loss of a child and are trying to reconcile how they move forward with hope and peace.

– CRISTIE NORTH

President, Taylor Hagen Memorial Foundation

———————————

It takes a special kind of person to walk through something so hard as your child taking their own life and publicly share it; and then to put your marriage and your life on display is simply heroic. Lark openly and in a very real and raw way shares the before, during, and after —all with the intent to hopefully assist others who find themselves having to navigate the same awful fate. I applaud truth tellers. The truth truly sets us free, and in these pages, Lark shares her deeply personal truths with us. Thank you, Lark.

– Kandy Graves
Pattern Breaking Energy Therapist; asyouthinkyouare.com

Lark's story is both heartbreaking and inspiring. She has experienced what most people would consider one of the most devastating losses a person can experience. She has created beauty from ashes as she shares her story to make a difference in the lives of others. Thank you, Lark, for your courage in sharing your grief and healing to assist us all in our journey through life.

– Julie Cluff
Grief Coach; buildalifeafterloss.com

LEARNING

Breathe

TO

AGAIN

LEARNING

Breathe TO

AGAIN

CHOOSING TO HEAL AFTER LOSING

A LOVED ONE TO SUICIDE

LARK DEAN GALLEY

DEDICATION

*For Christian, whose life's journey
has become intimately entwined with my own.
Thank you, Son, for your willingness to raise me
to a higher awareness.*

TABLE OF CONTENTS

FOREWORD

One summer evening, when I was twelve years old, I came home from a friend's house to find our foyer filled with people. As I was trying to figure out what was going on, my brother's girlfriend walked up to me.

"Why is everyone here?" I asked.

"Your mother slit her wrists," she said softly. "She's going to die."

My mother didn't die. But she didn't get better either. At least not emotionally. I remember at that time that we had an electric knife sharpener in the house. I couldn't tell you the name of my first-grade teacher, but I could draw a detailed picture of that knife sharpener. It was an avocado-colored can opener/knife-sharpener-in-one. It had a small doughnut-shaped magnet that held the can in place as you clamped down on it and a slightly sloped plastic appendage on its back with two small slits to run knife blades through.

Several times, in the weeks following her release from the hospital, my mother would go into the kitchen and sharpen a knife. The shriek of the blade against the grindstone could be heard anywhere in the house. I remember hiding behind the couch and covering my ears while each pass of the knife sent shivers through my body.

One night, after my mother had gone to bed, I stole the appliance. I wrapped it in a bath towel and hid it beneath the downstairs bathroom sink.

That wasn't the only time my mother attempted to take her life, and the fear of losing her loomed over my childhood like a specter. I don't know what effect those experiences had on me. I like to think that it taught me empathy. I like to believe that I'm a stronger man for it. But every now and then I feel those memories seep up through my thoughts like groundwater. And I realize that deep within me, there is still a shivering little boy covering his ears and hiding behind the couch.

While nearly a million people take their lives each year, the number of those affected, like the author of this book, are much higher. The profound emotional and psychological impact it has on those left behind in incalculable. You may be one of those carrying that enormous burden.

For this reason, it is important that society not only does what it can to understand those at risk of suicide but makes every attempt to reach out to those left wounded in its wake.

This book is an attempt to reach out. When I asked Lark Galley why she wanted to write this book, she said something profound. "It's something I felt I needed to do. It's not the mission I would have chosen, but it is the one I've been given."

This book might not have been the book Lark ever hoped to write, but it's the book we needed. And, for that reason, what I love even more than this book itself, is the fact that Lark found the strength to write it. In this we find evidence of not only courage, but hope.

That is what I hope you find in these pages. Courage and hope. Courage to live and love again. Hope to find joy again. May this book help you to that end.

– Richard Paul Evans
#1 *New York Times* bestselling author

Intro

THE NEWS

THERE ARE MOMENTS THAT CHANGE THE COURSE of your life. Those moments are so emotionally imprinted on your mind that you can instantly return to that very place—with the sights, sounds, and thoughts—when triggered by the memory.

My moment was Thursday, March 21, 2019 at 10 a.m. As the police officer entered the building I glanced at my watch and realized I had been teaching for an hour. Since I was only using the training room for the day and was not one of the normal tenants, I assumed he was here for someone else in the office.

"Can I help you?" I called out.

"Are you Lark Galley? Can we talk in private?" he said. Well, that's never a good thing for a police officer to say to you, but still I felt no worry or concern. I led him to an empty office in the back corner of the building.

"Please sit down," he said, pointing to the only available chair. Clearly, he was here to deliver some difficult news and thought I might faint or react poorly. He was about my height of five foot five, but he seemed much taller and definitely broader as I looked up at him from the chair. I got the impression of a kind man doing a tough job.

"I'm sorry to inform you that your son is dead."

I didn't respond. My mind went into denial and my heart closed. I displayed no emotion. Was what he was saying even possible? Christian couldn't be dead. Surely, the officer was mistaken. Christian had come home late last night after I'd gone to bed, and I had left early that morning. I hadn't seen him since yesterday morning when he headed off to school, but surely the officer was wrong.

The only thing I could think of was that he had been in a car accident on the way to the University of Utah where he was a freshman in the Engineering program. "Was it a car accident?" I asked.

"No. He shot himself at home," the officer answered.

Still I displayed no emotion. My mind raced to find a different interpretation of what he was saying. Suicide—the intentional taking one's life? That was even worse than a car accident, which offered some passivity and possible transfer of responsibility. Suicide spoke of a dark, empty hole that my husband and I were not even aware existed for our son.

I finally blurted out, "I'm sorry to appear so detached, but I'm in denial. I don't understand and cannot believe it's possible."

The officer kindly asked me, "Can you drive? Do you want to ride with me? We need you to come home right away."

Here's where the Ice Queen kicked in and my ability to completely isolate and compartmentalize my emotions took over. I had an obligation to the people who had traveled up to an hour to attend my class. I couldn't change anything at home. I would stick this horrible event—which clearly was a mistake—in the back compartment of my mind, lock the door, and deal with it later. This was my standard coping mechanism for dealing with troubling news.

"I can drive. I have to finish my class and can be home in two hours." The police officer could tell he was not getting through to me. "Your husband *needs* you at home. You need to come home now." Still in complete denial, I said, "Give me ten minutes to work with my co-host and I'll leave."

Looking back, I'm sure the officer thought I was a terrible wife and mother. What human on this planet is so detached and cold? It wasn't until several days later that I understood exactly why I had acted this way.

Chapter 1

SEEDS OF MENTAL ILLNESS

What mental health needs is more sunlight,
more candor, more unashamed conversation.

~ Glenn Close

My parents, Larry and Bevonne Dean, personified a typical young couple in the early 1960s. He was a full-time student and she had some post high school training in accounting before becoming a full-time homemaker. They were married at 22 and 21 respectively, and I was born 11 months later. We lived in a trailer in Provo, Utah near where my father attended school at Brigham Young University. His undergraduate degree was in English with a master's degree in Media Studies.

During this time, my parents had three other children in quick succession. My siblings were Emilie, Stephen, and Paul. We moved around to various nearby locations including an apartment behind a funeral home where part of the rent was paid by keeping the showroom tidy. I still have memories of myself as a young child playing on the floor while my pregnant mother dusted the caskets above me. Because of the time spent in the funeral home, and later living with my maternal grandparents behind a funeral home where my grandfather was the director, the associations many people have with death do not have the same negative connotations for me. Death and funerals were just a part of life, and I rarely cried at them, thinking those who had passed on were actually in a much better place and we were the ones to be pitied.

I have always had an adventurous spirit and would frequently head off exploring without telling my mom where I was going. Having two younger children made it difficult for her to keep up with me when we were living in Cedar City, Utah in the late 1960s, where my father was teaching at the high school. Mom begged him to move our family to the even smaller town of Kanarraville 13 miles south. At least here when I took off exploring, people would know where I belonged.

When I was five, we moved to the suburbs of Salt Lake City where I started kindergarten in the fall. During this time, my mom felt the all-too-familiar signs of pregnancy but noticed there was something different. Since she felt experienced in prenatal care and money was tight, she did not go to a doctor until she was seven months pregnant.

"Doc, I've done all the work up till now, so don't expect me to pay your full rate for delivery!" she told him in their first meeting. "Also, something seems to be different with this pregnancy. It could be twins."

Since she was measuring quite large for a normal baby, the doctor decided to take an X-ray. This was 1970 and not a normal procedure due to the potential harmful effects on the baby. It turned out my mom *was* experiencing an abnormal pregnancy. There wasn't just one baby or even two. There were three!

Later that evening when my father returned home from work, Mom said, "I went to the doctor today, and he took an X-ray. You're never going to believe it, but he says there are triplets!"

My dad turned pale. "What? Triplets? You're right, I don't believe it. I want that doctor's name and number because unless I hear it straight from him, I won't believe it."

The doctor put my mom on immediate bed rest. He didn't want any complications arising from an early delivery. This meant that from her bed, my mom had to care for four children aged five and under, with the youngest turning one the month before the babies were due. In hindsight, the bed rest seems a bit excessive as my mom was quite healthy and never experienced any problems during the pregnancy.

It was also during this time that my mom became acquainted with Velma Black, the mother of 11 children, the last two of which were twin girls. Velma was into natural foods and taught my mom about the negative effects of white flour and white sugar—both of which were immediately removed from our home, never to return. Additionally, we grew up with limited access to processed and fast foods. I blame my mom for instilling in me a hyper sense of nutrition, which prevents me from eating a Big Mac even in the face of severe hunger. It's also funny to think that our humble school lunches with her homemade, whole wheat bread would be quite trendy and popular today.

On December 22, 1970, my mother, who measured 44 inches around her waist, went into labor and delivered identical triplet girls—the likelihood of which I have seen placed at .003%. No, she was not on fertility drugs; in fact, she was actually using birth control. I think those girls were coming no matter what. They were full term and healthy, weighing in at a combined weight of 19 pounds of baby! Three days later, on Christmas Day, we picked them up from the hospital in cute Christmas stockings the nurses had made. The triplets' names were Kimberly, Kristine, and Kathleen, otherwise known as Kimmy, Krisie, and Kathy. We usually just called them Sissy or Trippies as they always seemed to be a collective rather than an individual.

The event was so unusual that our family had our picture and story in the local paper. Several people felt inclined to call the house and let my parents know what terrible people they were for unwittingly populating an already overcrowded world. I later reflected on their actions, thinking they had no idea what was actually going on in our home and wondering why they felt compelled to be so nasty about something that did not affect them directly in any way.

My dad was only 28 years old with seven children aged five and under. He felt a lot of pressure to provide for us as well as come to grips with his place in the world. I think this was a turning point in his life that we did not realize until several years later. As for my mother, she just rolled with the times and enjoyed her children even though there was a lot of work involved. I cannot imagine she got much sleep.

As the oldest, my sister and I were expected to pitch in with the work, including folding laundry, doing the dishes, and helping with the babies. It was all part of being a member of a large family, so we thought nothing of it until Grandma Dean's visit.

When Grandma saw four-year-old Emilie coming up the stairs with a full basket of laundry, she exclaimed, "What is she doing?" Clearly, Grandma thought us too young to be doing that kind of work, but I think my mom had her hands full.

The following year my dad decided to move our family across the country to Tennessee. He'd gotten a job at Columbia Community College, more to get away from his parents than anything else. Money was tight and he was good with his hands, so he built a custom camper for us to travel in. Besides my family, the camper held all our worldly possessions, which weren't much. I was the oldest at six and the triplets were the youngest at ten months. I was incredibly sad to leave my extended family of grandparents, aunts, uncles, and cousins, and felt my world being ripped away. Being separated by 1400 miles meant limited contact, as air travel and phone calls were then very pricey. This was during the fall, and school had already started, so I entered first grade as the new kid, in what was to become an annual occurrence.

Up until this time, church had been such a regular part of our life that I hardly have any distinct memories of it. This all changed

once we moved to Tennessee, where my father introduced our family to the small congregation.

"I'm Larry Dean, and this is my wife and seven children. They will probably be here regularly, but I will not."

This was the first time I can remember feeling different from other people, with a mother who went to church and a father who did not. Over the years my mother was diligent in getting her seven young children to church each Sunday. This would sometimes include an hour-long drive each way, tired and hungry kids, and running out of gas on more than one occasion. Her example instilled in me a deep conviction in doing what you thought was right even when it wasn't convenient. Another interesting reflection of this time is that I knew I could stay home with my father or attend church with my mother — it was my decision with no negative consequences either way.

Because I was allowed to choose, I attended church 99 percent of the time since that's where I wanted to be. With my independent nature and dislike of being told what to do, I wonder if I would have been so eager to attend if I had been forced to do so.

For the next decade, our family life would be chaotic and unstable. However, from my perspective as a child, my dad made it seem more like an adventure with lots of possibilities. He purchased a daycare center a couple of years after we moved to Tennessee. For the first several months our family slept together in the back room. There wasn't enough room for us to all have a bed, so the three oldest kids slept in hammocks. Like I said, my life felt like an adventure. What other kid slept in a hammock every night?

> *For the next decade our family life would be chaotic and unstable. Although, for a child, dad made it seem more like an adventure with lots of possibilities.*

Later my father had a two-bedroom mobile home placed behind the daycare center where we slept. Our family of nine used both bedrooms and the living room as sleeping areas. Since we had the entire center during the day with its toys and multiple activity areas, sleeping in a crowded space at night didn't seem too bad.

As with church, my father allowed us to choose whether or not we attended public school. He believed home schooling was the preferred education method, and while this might have proven true, that is not the case when no instruction is given to the home schooler other than self-directed learning.

The volatility in our home with my father's frequent job changes and our moving made it difficult for Emilie, who was more sensitive to her surroundings. She did not want to attend public school and was either placed in an alternative school or allowed to stay home for the first three years. This created a void in her educational foundation, for which she compensated, but could no longer be ignored in high school when my paternal grandmother ended up having to read her textbooks to her. As for me, I chose to stay home during third grade, which is when we owned the day care center. This proved to have the biggest impact on my inability to spell, which affected me greatly until auto correction became available.

The daycare center was growing and doing great until rumors started circulating that my father and one of the mothers were having an affair. In a small, religious Tennessee town, this was an economic disaster for a business. Parents started pulling their kids out of the school. Money had always been tight, but now it was impossible to pay the bills. To salvage whatever they could from the business, they held a fire sale to sell off any items from the school that could bring in some cash. We walked away with almost nothing, another recurring theme that was to show up throughout my life. As a side note, my mother never did confront my father about the affair, although she was quite sure it had occurred. Confrontation was not in her character.

My father decided to use my mother's knowledge and skill in the health food arena to open a trendy shop called Sutler's Loft. They offered herbs, eclectic antiques, and healthy foods. The idea was for my dad to run the shop and my mom to stay home to raise the children, but my mom was soon running the shop full time when my dad's restless demons took over and he felt compelled to move on. He told my mom the only place he could find a job was as a teacher in Arizona. Keep in mind we lived in Franklin, Tennessee. I'm certain there were a few teaching jobs somewhere in the area, but the need for adventure and change was calling.

"I've decided to take a teaching job in North Eastern Arizona for the next school year," he told her late that summer. "I'll take the two boys with me, so you won't have to keep all the kids."

At the last minute, my mom said to me, "Will you go with dad to keep an eye on the boys? I'm really concerned about them being so far away." It was rather a heavy responsibility for a ten- year-old, and I felt the weight of it.

During this time, my brothers and I had some crazy adventures in Arizona. Our father would take us to spend the weekend at the Indian reservations so he could film the pow wows. We would stay up late watching the dancing and then sleep in the back of our Chevy Suburban.

At home we were often left to our own devices and had the Fire Marshall visit us twice for neighbor complaints of unauthorized fires. I clearly remember my father answering the door, listening to the Fire Marshall, then turning him over to me and leaving the room. Clearly my father did not take much responsibility as a parent for what we chose to do.

One night in the fall my dad announced, "I'm going to a movie tonight, but it's not appropriate for you kids."

"Please, Dad, please let us go!" We didn't have a TV and could rarely afford a movie, so this sounded like a real treat.

Dad resisted a little but finally relented. Off we went to the local movie theater to watch *The Exorcist*. He was right, it was not appropriate for kids. Afterwards I lived in fear that I would be possessed and was afraid to turn the lights off at night. My youngest brother Paul, who was not quite five, wouldn't go into a room by himself for years, regardless of whether it was day or night. Clearly, another parenting fail on my dad's part.

Even though my dad said he would send money home to my mom, I doubt he did, because we never seemed to have enough for ourselves. Toward the end of each pay period, we always ended up eating lunch at home rather than in the school cafeteria because we didn't have the money. This was easy to do since the elementary we attended, and the high school where my father taught, were all within a short walking distance. We also needed to save money on utilities. I don't think my dad ever turned on the heater. Since we lived at a higher elevation it was often cold at night. I would compensate for the lack of heat by sleeping in my coat.

We drove back home to Tennessee for the Christmas break, and my parents decided the Arizona fling had come to an end. My dad quit the teaching job and put his master's degree in media to use working for the owner of the trendy shopping center, creating advertising to bring in tourists. This was the same shopping center where my mom's health food store was located.

During our time in Arizona, my mom had moved into an old, two-bedroom one-bath house within a ten-minute walk of the shopping center. Since money was tight, she often left my sister, Emilie, age nine, to watch over the triplets, age four, while she worked. All seven kids ended up sleeping in the bigger bedroom, with my parents in the smaller, second bedroom. There was no fan and certainly no air-conditioning. I remember waking up on several nights that summer completely drenched in sweat.

In our absence, my mom had done well with Sutler's Loft. She had created a great lunch clientele and was finally operating in the black. A few months after moving back from Arizona, my parents also took over the ice cream store that was in the same shopping center. It always struck me as funny that we were running two completely opposing businesses. Once school let out for the summer, my sister Emilie helped my mom in the health food store, and I helped my dad in the ice cream store.

My dad would open the ice cream store, then walk over to the office for his advertising job. At the age of eleven,

I would run the place by myself from 10 a.m. until noon when another lady would come in to help me with the lunch and afternoon crowd. Besides getting paid five dollars for the entire day, I also got to eat as much ice cream as I wanted. Clearly this was a better deal than working in the health food shop. With the adults and older girls working, this left my brothers and triplets at home by themselves for most of the day during the summer.

I started sixth grade and can remember being unable to read the chalkboard despite having glasses and sitting in the front row. My dad took us kids in for eye checkups. We all got new glasses, but because we qualified for low income assistance, they were the ugliest pairs imaginable. Think of the large, black glasses with a mustache attached that you might find at a joke shop. Emilie actually cried at the thought of having to wear the hideous things.

Dad said, "No one will notice, and if anyone makes fun of your glasses, I'll give you a quarter."

This is what coaxed us to start wearing them, although I don't recall our ever remembering to ask Dad for the quarter, despite being made fun of by the other kids.

My parent's relationship began to deteriorate again that fall. My father's undiagnosed bipolarity would manifest itself in spurts of excitement and grand ideas, only to be followed by weeks of depression and isolation. My mom told me later of their conversation late one night.

As they were lying in bed, Dad said, "I think I should take Emilie, Stephen, and Kim, and leave. Those three are the most vulnerable and need extra support. We'll take off and you'll never hear from us again."

Dad's surprising declaration shows he had no idea how unstable he was. If these three children were the most vulnerable and in need of extra support, they should have been with the more stable parent. This was not my father.

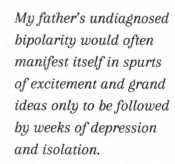

My father's undiagnosed bipolarity would often manifest itself in spurts of excitement and grand ideas only to be followed by weeks of depression and isolation.

Dad's declaration terrified my mother because in 1976, disappearing from society was a very real possibility. She was 2,000 miles from her parents, had no resources, and seven children to care for. Even without a bipolar diagnosis, she must have known something was wrong with her husband.

My mom was so concerned my father would actually carry out this new fantasy that she started to make her own plan. In early December, she pulled Emilie and me aside. We were both still in elementary school but had experienced so much together that we were considered much older than the other kids. It says a lot that she trusted us with her secret.

"Girls, we're leaving on Friday for my parents' house in Southern California. You cannot tell your Dad or the other kids. You also cannot pack much, or dad will suspect something."

When she checked us out early from school, we each had the equivalent of one orange box with all we possessed inside. She made a mad dash across the country to her parents, sleeping only a few hours at rest stops when absolutely necessary. We didn't have much money, so she brought several food items from the health food shop that we ate along the way.

We arrived just before Christmas with only what the Suburban could hold, which was Mom, seven kids, our clothes, and a mattress in the back to sleep on. If it hadn't been for my grandparents, aunts, and uncles, it would have been a very bleak holiday for us kids.

We spent the second half of my sixth-grade year in Southern California. I remember thinking to myself as I stood with my mom waiting to register at the new school, "I have another clean slate. I can be who I want." Then the voice of awareness answered, "No, your personality is set. You are who you are and no amount of trying to squash that person is going to work."

Without mom in Tennessee to run Sutler's Loft, my dad ended up closing the store and selling off what assets he could. He also sold the ice cream store and had a fire sale on any of the household items we'd left behind. I didn't have much, but I wondered who got my little metal bookshelf, as it was the only piece of furniture I owned.

My parents worked on their marriage long distance. By the end of the summer, they decided to get back together. My grandparents drove back with us to Tennessee in their camper, so at least we had two vehicles instead of one to spread out in.

By this time, my father had quit his job as the advertising specialist for the shopping center and struck out on his own. He found a nice house for rent outside Nashville in the upscale neighborhood of Brentwood. When we arrived and took a tour of the house, I remember thinking, "Wow! This is too fancy for us." We had never lived in anything so nice in our lives. There were four bedrooms, which meant I wasn't sleeping with all six siblings.

I was once again starting at a new school, but this time the stakes seemed to be higher because it was junior high. Despite the nice house, there wasn't much money. New school clothes were not often in the family budget, and this time was no exception. My grandmother was still with us from the trip out from California. She was a seamstress and had often sewn her own clothes. She took a pair of my old pants that still fit me around the waist but not the length, and cut off two sections at the bottom of each leg. She then sewed material between the sections, thereby lengthening the pants enough to reach my shoes. While I wasn't thrilled, I was happy to have another pair of pants to add to my ridiculously small wardrobe.

I had the misfortune of wearing these pants on a Thursday, which was the day I crossed the road from the junior high to the senior high for my music class. There was one very tall boy who decided to make fun of my pants. As we crossed the road, he shouted loudly for all to hear, "Look at her pants! She's just going to keep extending them for the rest of her life." I was mortified. I vowed right then that I would change my circumstances so I would never be ridiculed for my clothes again. I also started developing a very thick skin and became immune to many of the snide comments the other kids would make about me or my family.

We lived here for about eight months. I made some friends; although, once again, my family remained fairly isolated. I attended a girlfriend's birthday party where they played spin the bottle. This was a very new experience for me, and at twelve years old, I was not comfortable. I chose to sit that one out. Fortunately, there was another girl who chose to do the same, so I didn't feel extremely awkward— just a little bit awkward. There was also slow dancing in the dark. I chose to watch over the record player rather than risk that uncomfortable situation. I was not cute and didn't know many of the people in the room. It was obvious that I was the outsider in the group.

One Friday evening in the early spring, my dad came home from a road trip to Virginia where he'd been interviewing for a new job. He sat us kids down on the floor and pulled out a map. He then showed us where we lived in Tennessee and where we were going to be living—tomorrow. We were to pack up our stuff that night as he was getting a U-Haul in the morning and we were out of there.

I also realize my dad's continual need for adventure overrode any level of personal responsibility he might have taken to provide a stable environment for his family.

He made it all sound like a huge adventure, which got us excited. There was even the possibility for "Dean's Donkey Ranch" on the remote property where we would be living.

Looking back on it now, I can only think what a huge liability that would have been. I also realize my dad's continual need for adventure overrode any level of personal responsibility he might have taken to provide a stable environment for his family.

Other than our bedroom furniture, clothes, Dad's desk, and a long, skinny kitchen table that my father had built so my mom could easily reach across to help the small children, we owned very little. I don't even think we had a couch. My possessions once again fit easily into an orange box. My one concern was my school binder that was still in my locker. It was nice, and I felt sad that I couldn't retrieve it before we left. It should speak volumes about our financial situation that I fretted over leaving a school binder because I might not get another one.

We moved into an older home in the very small town of Warm Springs, Virginia. Dad was working a few hours away on a dam construction project. Because we only had one vehicle, he convinced Mom that his hitch-hiking to and from work, coming home only on the weekends, was the best thing for the family. During the week he stayed in the man camp, which I'm sure fulfilled his dreams for adventure—at least temporarily.

I finished seventh grade there and made several friends. I had the reputation of not participating in the Cooties game which the other students would inflict on David Pendergrass. He was a larger boy who was a bit slow, but I couldn't see the point in making fun of someone. I'd been on the receiving end of that stick too many times.

I do remember the year-end tests we were required to take because a strange situation occurred. Rather than sit in the classroom with the other students, I was asked by the teacher to take my test separately. My test was to be taken in a small room with another student. This boy, James, had already been held back two years. For him to move on to the eighth grade, he had to pass this comprehensive test. The problem was, he couldn't read. I was to read the questions out loud, then we were to mark our answers separately. This blew me away for two reasons. First, how could someone who was fifteen not know how to read? I was not aware of Emilie's own reading situation at the time. Second, why weren't the teachers or his parents more involved in helping this boy, who would clearly be at a disadvantage if he didn't learn basic reading skills? I'm sure he felt extremely awkward during the tests, but I tried to make him as comfortable as possible through the whole process.

That summer we moved thirty minutes away to the slightly larger town of Covington, Virginia. I started high school because eighth grade was held in the same building. Once again, I made some friends, but we were so isolated I don't remember anyone other than the neighbor girl coming to visit. Few friends and no TV meant I spent a lot of time reading. I preferred to escape into someone else's world rather than face the lack in my own.

We lasted here only about four months before my parents decided to move back to Utah. I was 13, and this was my sixth move across the U.S. While this might not be remarkable for military families, it certainly was odd for a family that didn't actually have to move every six to twelve months. It was only when I entered the workforce as an adult and experienced this same restlessness and craving for the unknown that I began to understand my father's need to move so often.

Back in Utah, we were surrounded once again by my extended family. Except for the few months in Southern California, this was something I'd been without for the past seven years. In an attempt to mitigate his mother's influence on our family, Dad moved us to the small town of Morgan. He found a tiny, cheap, two-bedroom one-bath house for the nine of us to live in. To create more space, he built a sleeping loft over the small living room where my five younger siblings would climb a ladder to sleep on mattresses in sleeping bags.

With only one bathroom, we had to be very efficient in the mornings to get ready for school. This meant co-ed bathroom use with one sibling on the toilet, one at the sink, and one in the shower in rotating fashion. Family togetherness at its finest.

My father found work in Salt Lake City, ninety minutes southwest of where we lived. In order to avoid commuting every day, he stayed with his parents in their nice home during the week and only came home to the hovel on the weekends. He actually bragged to the church congregation about spending so little on his family.

"Everyone keeps talking about how smart it is to own your own place, but I only pay $125 a month for our rent. It's a better deal because I have no extra expenses on upkeep," Dad told the adult Sunday School class.

His eccentricities seemed to magnify as he felt the need to publicly proclaim his disenchantment with societal norms and expectations, which only caused me to isolate more from others from sheer embarrassment.

Dad getting ready to lower the younger kids off a cliff into an eagle's nest. Not much safety equipment or back up plan if things went wrong, but always an adventure.

I turned 14 here and remember my mom mixing the powdered milk with real milk to extend it. I would always beg her not to mix the milk so at least we had some milk that tasted good versus all of it tasting bad. She never did.

I was recently reminded by my friend, Linda, who knew me at that time, how Emilie and I would hide bread in our room to make sure we had it for our lunches. Since this doesn't stand out to me, it must have been a regular occurrence. I do remember having limited food choices. I also remember my mom giving plasma to earn a few extra dollars to buy groceries.

I made several friends in Morgan and, for the first time, started spending time with them after school. A friend came to my house one day, not a normal occurrence, and later Emilie asked, "How could you invite someone over? Aren't you embarrassed that we live so poorly?"

This had never occurred to me, and I said, "My friend is coming to see *me*, not the house, and if she has a problem with the house, I probably didn't want to be her friend anyway."

During this year, I also participated on the volleyball, basketball, and track teams which gave me additional social interaction with others. I was friendly but still very much the awkward kid. I started working first with a paper route and later as a busboy at the local diner. Earning fifty dollars a month made me feel ultra-rich and allowed me to buy my own clothes, which helped a lot with the self-image.

My dad's undiagnosed mental illness really started manifesting itself during this time. First, he was obsessed with sexual promiscuity. We once had a private talk about any desires I might have toward having sex with some-one, which to him was totally okay; I just needed to talk with him first so he could make sure I had birth control. What was even stranger was when I asked him two weeks later for permission to go with a group of friends to watch the older boys play hockey late at night, I was told, "Your mother and I wouldn't want you doing that." The message I heard was, "You can have sex, but we don't want you hanging out with a group of friends late at night." It was very confusing to me and created a lot of mental conflict as to what was acceptable.

The message I heard was, you can have sex, but we don't want you hanging out with a group of friends late at night.

Other times that had my sister and me wanting to die of shame was when my father would attend church with us. He seemed to only want to go on the first Sunday of the month when they have the equivalent of "open mic night." He couldn't pass up the opportunity to tell our congregation of 200 plus how cheaply we lived, what various personal issues the family was going through, and how the teenagers were embarrassed to be seen in the old car that the neighboring family had donated to us. Clearly, he needed a lot of attention and was willing to let his children pay the price for his unfiltered comments.

My parents continued to struggle in their marriage. It was as if we kids knew divorce was inevitable, but our parents couldn't bring themselves to do it. Toward the end of my ninth- grade year, Dad took the whole family to see the movie *Kramer vs. Kramer* about a couple who decided to get divorced.

After the movie, Dad broke the news. "Kids, your mom and I are getting a divorce. We don't regret getting married because we had you, which made it all worthwhile."

Hallelujah! At least the craziness of pretending things could work out would finally stop.

With the divorce came another move. We had lived in Morgan for 18 months—the longest I've ever lived anywhere, so it was hard to leave. We packed the U-Haul and headed to Logan where Mom and the kids would live close to her sister. Dad would continue to live in Salt Lake City near his stable job. Mom got a full-time job, but the money was still tight. I remember our diet was very basic, with meat only being served on Sunday, when we would have a special chicken dinner after church.

Dad was a dreamer and adventurer and had a hard time being tied down to family life for any length of time. In the divorce decree, he was now required to pay child support, which necessitated maintaining a job. Mom told me, "This has been the most stable period of his career as he can't jump around whenever he gets bored."

I would classify my tenth-grade year as one of the hardest. The kids at the school were divided into a lot of cliques. While they probably wouldn't think of themselves as excluding others, I felt like an outsider most of the time. I was friendly and able to form some acquaintances within these groups, but I had few close friends. I was still the socially awkward one in the room. Looking back, I can see where I started to isolate both physically and emotionally. The seeds of my Ice Queen personality started early on as I tried to shield our family's instability from the world.

Our first house in Logan had three bedrooms and one

bathroom for the eight of us to share. Mom had joined Amway in the hopes of earning some additional income, but the only thing it got us were motivational tapes, which she played continually during our morning bathroom time. As a 15-year-old, I thought she was subjecting me to the worst torture imaginable.

"Mom, please turn off those awful tapes and let us listen to the radio!" I begged.

But she wouldn't stop. Every day I was subjected to a barrage of positive mental attitude stories, told to me in a Southern accent. I listened so often, I started thinking in Southern. Slowly my mind started to expand to new possibilities, and I realized other people were worse off than I was, and that if they could turn their life around, surely I could too.

It was during this time that I was introduced to the idea of going on foreign exchange, which involves living with a family and attending school in another country. While this idea today might not seem so farfetched, I can promise you that in 1980, I might as well have been going to the moon. Thanks to the new mindset I had acquired from Mom's MPA tapes, a lot of hard work, and several miracles, I was able to stay with the Ollas family who lived outside Stockholm, Sweden for my junior year.

I remember walking into their beautiful home for the first time. It was spacious with only four people living in the house. For the first time in my life, I had my own private bedroom. There was a bedspread that was color coordinated with the furniture and wallpaper. It was so lovely I almost started to cry and caught myself before blurting out, "Oh, is this really mine?"

I finally felt what a normal life could be like. They had stability. They had enough food. They had heat. We actually conversed over dinner, where they took an interest in my activities.

"So, Lark, your family has lived in several different places. How many times have you moved?" my Swedish father, Arne, asked one evening, and was shocked at my answer.

"I'm not exactly sure, but I think it's over thirty times," I said. Since I was only sixteen, that averages to more than twice a year.

My experience on exchange had a profound effect on me and the direction of my life. Suddenly, I knew I wanted a different future.

The instability in my life affected me in several ways. First, I determined that I would never be poor. This was a driving force in getting my education and moving up within my career. My children would never suffer the stigma of wearing old clothes, glasses that were so ugly you wanted to cry, and socks and underwear with holes. Additionally, my children would learn to play a musical instrument, have long-term friendships, and know they had food in the cupboard.

Another way I unknowingly coped with my upbringing and history of family mental illness was to create extremely strict habits and patterns. I needed order in my life to deal with the slightly crazy voices in my head. Everything had to be just so. This was partly what created such a rift between me and my son. He could never understand why I needed the house to be tidy and calm. He often accused me of being OCD when it came to cleanliness. What neither he nor I knew was that my need for control stemmed from years of my having so little control in a very tumultuous upbringing. I didn't fully understand this until years later when I heard my sister, Kim, make a comment to my father.

"How come Lark missed the crazy train?" she asked.

"Lark hasn't missed it. She's just learned to cope with the crazy by living a highly structured life," Dad said.

As I reflected on his statement, I realized he was right. I would always intentionally have a project underway in order to keep my mind focused and present; otherwise, I could feel myself start to spiral into depression.

My father had always shown signs of bipolarity, but it wasn't diagnosed until he was in his early fifties. It turned out that his mother and grandmother had also struggled with their mental health; however, unlike his illness, theirs went undiagnosed their entire lives. The mental illness was passed down not only to my father, but also to some of his siblings, several of my siblings, and several cousins. One cousin even passed away from an unintentional overdose in an attempt to cope with his illness. While I watched for any signs of mental illness in my children, I never noticed any. It wasn't until my

It wasn't until my son's passing that I realized his heightened sensitivity to others' feelings was one sign I'd missed. I used to joke that he was more sensitive than his sisters. It doesn't seem like much of a joke now.

son's passing that I realized his heightened sensitivity to others' feelings was one sign I'd missed. I used to joke that he was more sensitive than his sisters. It doesn't seem like much of a joke now.

Chapter 2

THE FOUNDATION

---

*Thy servant slew both the lion and the bear: and
this uncircumcised Philistine shall be as one of them,
seeing he hath defied the armies of the living God.*

~ SAMUEL 17:36 KJV

THE BIBLE STORY OF DAVID AND GOLIATH is a wonderful
example of God's ability to help us overcome significant
odds and come out on top. Yet one particularly important piece which comes before the "big event" and lays the
groundwork for David's absolute faith in God's ability to
protect and provide is often ignored. This missing piece
is David's recounting of both a lion and a bear coming to
steal his father's sheep and how he killed them both. Now
a giant can seem scary, but honestly, I think a lion and
a bear might make me even more afraid. Can you even
imagine facing something like that in our world today—a
real, tangible threat to your life, not just some emotional

devastation? Yet while those encounters must have been frightening for David, they were necessary in order for him to stand before Saul with complete confidence in God's ability to deliver him from Goliath.

As we go through the early stages of life, we might face a trial that we think of as our Goliath—our biggest trial to overcome before moving on to a glorious end. However, what we might initially think of as our Goliath is really our lion or bear coming to prepare us for the impending Goliath. How young and naïve we are. That's the way it was for me. What I thought was my Goliath was actually just my lion preparing me for what was to come.

My lion came in my late twenties. After three years of marriage, I decided it was time to get pregnant. I had a prenatal check up with my doctor and told her how my timing would fit nicely into my life plan.

"Doc, I've got it all figured out. I'm going off birth control this month and will be pregnant by next month."

She started laughing hysterically and said, "You know, that's not necessarily the way it works."

Later, as I progressed through three years of unexplained infertility and read many articles on this "streamlined" process, I was shocked at the complexity of the conception process and thought, "It's actually a miracle anyone gets pregnant at all!"

During the time I was trying to get pregnant, I was living and working in the San Francisco Bay Area as a sales rep in the global logistics industry. My husband, whose father was Portuguese and worked for their government's Foreign

Service, grew up all over the world. We only happened to meet because his parents sent him to attend school and live with a family in Utah. His ability to speak Portuguese allowed him special status with United Airlines, where he worked as a flight attendant on their New York to Brazil route. He would deadhead from San Francisco in the morning, arriving in New York in time to work his shift on the redeye to Brazil. He was gone for five days at a time about three times a month. This sounds like only part time, but it actually felt like we were separated a lot more because when he was home I was working during the day, and when I was home at night he was often away. As our lives continued with this pattern, I felt very lonely, since all my family was back in Utah.

After unsuccessfully trying to get pregnant through my OBGYN, I started going to the Palo Alto Infertility Clinic, which had some of the best infertility specialists in the nation. After a year of various tests on both my husband and me, my specialist finally said, "I can't find anything amiss with either your husband's or your ability to procreate. You just don't seem to be able to do it together. You do realize that being in the same room is a prerequisite to getting pregnant, right?"

Being in the same room was often difficult due to our schedules, and the unromantic and non-spontaneous encounters we did have seemed forced and unfulfilling to our marriage. Yet for the sake of our family, we persisted, even going so far as to have two unsuccessful rounds of in vitro. The hormones I was required to inject during this time had me on a train wreck of emotions. Add to this the compounding lone-liness, and you will begin to understand my emotional state.

This experience with infertility was critical to my devel-oping a closer relationship with God. For most of my life I had been in charge and able to accomplish whatever goal I chose, but conceiving a child was not in my control. As the months passed, I recognized my complete dependence on Him. My prayers were a plea to grant me my righteous desire to be a mother. Wasn't that a good thing? Hadn't I kept His commandments? Didn't I deserve this blessing? On and on it went, to the point where He actually told me "No" during my prayers, yet I wouldn't accept it. I continued with the shots and infertility treatment thinking, "I'll show you. I'll do it myself if I have to."

Around my 30th birthday and after three years of unsuc-cessful attempts to get pregnant, I was emotionally and phys-ically washed up. Our medical insurance had also reached the point where the next step, artificial insemination, was not covered. Our choice was to spend $10,000 for a possible pregnancy or $10,000 on adoption for a guaranteed child. I chose the latter and set up an appointment with the adop-tion agency. A couple of days before my appointment, I real-ized my period was late and that I was starting to show the beginning signs of pregnancy. I was ecstatic and canceled my appointment with the adoption agency.

I took a pregnancy test, which came out positive, and was planning the nursery. A few weeks later I started spot-ting. My doctor had me go in for an ultrasound where they discovered a blighted ovum, which means the egg was empty and would be naturally aborted. I was devastated, but I also experienced great feelings of hope. I had at least gotten pregnant which was a big, first step. If it had happened once, it could happen again.

A few months later another pregnancy test came out positive. I was ecstatic. When my husband returned from a work trip, I excitedly sat him down in the living room and said, "I'm pregnant!" Never could I have imagined his response. "Well, I don't want to be a father, and I don't want to be married to you." I was completely blindsided. Yes, we struggled a bit due to our schedules, but hadn't we been house hunting in preparation for our baby?

Thus began 18 months of depression as I struggled through the grief and death of my marriage. My husband tried every possible tactic to anger or demean me, thereby hoping to justify his position. In addition to being emotional from the pregnancy, I was battling the dissolution of what I thought had been a good marriage. Had I been so deluded and unaware that I could have missed something? When I was six months pregnant, he walked out, leaving no forwarding address or telephone number. This was before the ubiquitous use of cell phones.

Thus began 18 months of depression as I struggled through the grief and death of my marriage.

Two things got me through his very dark time. The first was the relationship with God I had forged while going through my infertility. My reliance on Him became complete as I struggled to cope with the abandonment and disintegration of my foundation and all the expectations I had for our future.

I had several insights revealed to me about God's love for me and the child I was carrying. I came to know that no matter what the circumstances were, God would always be there to support me through my difficulties. I once had a church leader ask if I blamed God for what happened with my marriage. I laughed and said, "Why would I do that? He had nothing to do with my husband's leaving. That was his choice."

The second thing that got me through my absolute despair was my daughter. She was the only bright spot in an otherwise bleak future. I was grateful that something beautiful had come from something so painful. She was the reason I retained any desire to move forward with my life.

What I thought was a tragedy at the time turned out to be a blessing. My first husband's leaving allowed me to meet and marry a man who was solid in his commitments as a husband and father. Additionally, not getting pregnant on my timetable ensured there was no bond between father and daughter. He walked away without a backward glance, which allowed me total custody and no interference on his part.

When my daughter, Skye, was 14 months old, I married Stephen Galley. After the required year of marriage, Stephen was able to adopt her. He is the only father she has ever wanted or needed. Both Stephen and his widowed mother, Kathy, completely loved and accepted Skye as if she had been his biological child, which was a great example to me of unconditional love. This example would come into play 20 years later in a most unexpected way when Caleb entered our lives.

Chapter 3

CHRISTIAN'S EARLY YEARS

If nobody's dying, it's a good day.

~ STEPHEN GALLEY
UPON HIS RETURN FROM AFGHANISTAN

TWO YEARS AFTER STEPHEN AND I WERE MARRIED, we had a son. The best way to describe Christian is that he was unique. He danced to the beat of his own drum and was content to live by his own set of rules. My earliest memory of his abilities is when I would sing to him while nursing. Granted, I am not the best of singers, but it certainly didn't help my ego to have my four-month old reach up to close my lips whenever I tried to sing a lullaby to him. Later we discovered he had an excellent musical ear, which helped him learn how to play the violin, piano, guitar, and compose his own songs.

As Christian neared the age of two, I began to worry about his ability to communicate. While he spoke one or two words at a time, he had yet to speak a full sentence. My coworker's young child was struggling with his speech and seeing a speech therapist for help. With Christian's lack of complete sentences, I thought he might need to see a speech therapist as well. I resigned myself to having a child who might be a bit slower in his development.

Then one night that all changed. As we sat at the dinner table, my son wiped his mouth with his napkin. He continued to eat and then reached for his napkin again. As he brought it up to his mouth, he noticed some food left on the napkin from his earlier swipe and said, "Oh, that's disgusting!" For the first sentence, that was pretty impressive. Suddenly, my life brightened as I realized my son might not be mentally challenged.

Christian idolized his daddy and wanted to be with him all the time. Dad was in the military, so Christian saw him as an authority figure and picked up on the alpha male hierarchy early on. Being the only other male in the house, he thought that placed him right behind dad in the pecking order. One evening after a long day at work, I stood at the kitchen sink, cleaning up the dinner dishes. I asked Christian to do a small task. He would have been about three at the time because I can clearly remember him wearing a Pull-up without a shirt as he stood up on the chair, pointed at me with his skinny arm, and said loudly, "You can't tell me what to do! Only Daddy can tell me what to do!"

That was the moment I learned the meaning of the phrase "seeing red" as the blood crept up behind my eyes. I turned toward my son with only one thought in my mind, "Kill the boy!" As I moved toward him with arms outstretched, his father, who had heard the exchange, vaulted over the couch, stepping between us, to prevent me from getting to him. Turning his head to look at Christian he simply said, "Son, do what your mom asked now!" Thus began the pattern for our future interactions, I with my son questioning and challenging everything I said.

By the time Christian was five years old, his very logical mind enabled him to argue like a seasoned defense attorney. He loved to debate whatever request I put forth and could usually lay out a very eloquent sequence as to why I was wrong and he was right. Every day after work as I entered the day care, I promised myself that today I would have patience and would not allow anything he said to upset me. Every day I broke that promise as we often wouldn't even make it out of the parking lot before I was furious with some statement he made about my incompetence for not completing a task or request he had made earlier.

Skye had started the Suzuki violin method when she was three years old. I waited until Christian was four and his younger sister, Victoria, was three before starting them, so I could help them with their practice at the same time. As mentioned earlier, Christian had a great ear for music and could do quite well when he chose. Over the years we

struggled through several teachers before finding one that could work with his unique personality.

When Victoria was five, I started her on piano lessons. I was willing to give Christian a pass on learning two instruments, but throughout the year he would listen to Victoria play and then go play the same song himself. I realized he had a lot of natural talent, and I started him in formal lessons. He preferred to play by ear and was a bit lazy about reading the notes. By the time he was a teenager, he started composing his own music for his recitals and said, "I write my own songs so no one can tell me I'm playing it wrong." This seemed like even more work than just learning to play the song as it was written, but if that's what it took to have him stick with it, so be it.

When Christian turned 14, he said, "Mom, enough with the two instruments. I want to drop the violin."

"Son, I'm sorry to hear it, but if you'll continue with the piano, we'll agree to have you stop with the violin lessons."

The year Christian entered first grade, I counted the days before his teacher called. She made it to day three.

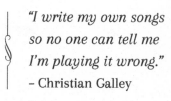

"Hello, Mrs. Galley. This is Christian's first grade teacher. I am so sorry to be contacting you, but could I talk with you about your son?"

I started to laugh and replied, "I'm just surprised you made it to day three as I've been expecting your call since the first day." As many of his teachers have said over the years, "Christian won't do what we ask, but he's always very polite about it."

Finding ways for corrective discipline proved challenging, as Christian was not hampered by much. When I told him he had timeout in his room he would reply, "Great! I'm going to play with my Legos." When I told him he had lost his treats for the day his optimistic response was, "Well, there's always tomorrow!" How was I going to discipline this boy?

That Christmas Christian received a dinosaur erector set which he immediately started putting together. He spent the entire day working on it and had almost completed it when he took a break. Dad then decided to help and began working on the neck and head, which proved to be a complete botch job. Christian was so furious that he had to take apart everything Stephen had done that he banned Dad from helping on any more of his projects. The six-year-old proved to have better mechanical and spatial skills than his father.

A story that illustrates how Christian's mind worked is when I took my three kids and their five cousins to the zoo. Rather than haul all eight of them across the long parking lot to the car, I put eight-year-old Skye in charge and told them all to wait right by the waterfall. This was a beautiful area with water cascading over the rocks settling down below in a pool where people had thrown money like a wishing well. Before heading to the car, I looked specifically at Christian, knowing exactly where he would end up and said, "Do not get wet!"

Guess where I found him when I pulled up five minutes later? Down in the water pit, standing on a rock in the middle of the pool, picking up the money.

"Christian, what are you doing? I told you not to get in the water!"

"But Mom, I didn't get wet," he answered honestly.

"Well, you can't keep the money, so put it back and climb out," I told him. Obviously, I should have been more specific about not climbing on the rocks or going down into the pool.

Christian's innate ability to visualize in 3-D manifested itself early on. His favorite way to spend his free time was building with Legos. He could literally spend eight hours straight completely engrossed. While he could put together the Lego sets per the kit instructions, he enjoyed coming up with his own designs even more. When he was about nine, he designed and built a triple combination locking safe with moving parts. This was not from a kit but completely from his imagination. Around this same time, he became involved with Lego Robotics and was on a local team that competed at the State level. He loved being part of this group.

The spring of 2006 brought some serious changes and heartache into our home as Stephen's Utah Guard unit was activated to Afghanistan for 18 months. I had often thought of the sacrifices that soldiers make when serving our country. I was about to learn firsthand the sacrifices the family left behind were required to make.

I was working a rigorous corporate job which often required me to be gone for long hours. My mother, who was a widow from her second husband's passing, was kind enough to agree to live with us. I wouldn't have made it without her help. She would ensure the kids got off to school and was home when they returned in the afternoon. She often prepared dinner before sailing out the door as I returned home at night to take over. With Stephen gone, I felt like a single parent as I tried to be all things to our kids.

Christian was six when his father left for Afghanistan. Stephen's telling him that he was now "the man of the house and had to take care of the girls" only strengthened his alpha male perceptions. There were a few times within the first week of Stephen's leaving that I had to assert my authority quite forcefully. These times included my response to Christian's statement that "Dad left me in charge" or "Mom, this isn't your house, it's Dad's."

I also realized Christian's understanding of how marriage and parenting worked was not fully developed when he announced, "Mom, if Dad is killed in Afghanistan, you're going to need to get remarried, so I can have a daddy to play with."

"That's not how it works, son. No one could ever take your daddy's place, and I don't think anyone is going to love you as much as he does."

That fall, when school started, Christian's fear for his father's safety started manifesting itself. He would often claim he was sick or make himself throw up at school, so he could stay home. After a few of these incidents happened close together, I realized what was going on and had a stern talking with him. Dad even had to call home to have a talk with Christian.

Sometime during this school year, an announcement was made over the intercom that there would be an assembly and brief memorial honoring a soldier who had been killed in Afghanistan and whose children were in the school. Skye, who was nine at the time, sat quietly for a while before finally having the courage to walk up and ask her teacher, "Was someone going to tell me that my father's been killed?"

"Oh, Skye! I am so sorry. It was not your father," her teacher cried out in horror. Needless to say, there had been a terrible misunderstanding. There was a soldier who had died, but what the school failed to realize was that there were multiple fathers of children in the school who were serving at that time. The school never made this mistake again.

Something that helped the kids during this time was the Daddy Bear dressed in an Army uniform they created at Build a Bear. One of them carried it with them whenever we went on trips or activities as a way to keep Dad close. They were also involved with UTNG Kids which provided activities for children of Utah Guard members. After attending several of these activities Christian told me, "I really appreciate the Guard Kids program because it's the only place I can go where there are other kids whose parents are deployed. None of my other friends understand what it's like for me to have my dad gone."

When Stephen had been deployed for almost a year, he came home for his two-week break. These breaks are quick without any buffer time as the soldier comes out of theater. As I was driving him home from the airport, he sat in the passenger seat with his head on a swivel.

"Hey, big guy, there are no snipers here," I jokingly said since I could see he was on the lookout.

"Watch out for that car coming up on the left! Force him off the road! Force him off the road!" he yelled.

"Stephen, we do not force cars off the road here. There is no danger here," I told him calmly as I placed my hand on his arm. I began to get a glimpse into the total lack of safety he had been exposed to. Here we were at home going about our lives as if others in the world weren't in constant fear for theirs.

It was great having Dad home during this short break, which ended all too quickly. The night before Stephen returned, he packed his duffel bag, leaving just a space on top for his toiletry kit. Once he was back at his Afghan base, he dumped out the contents on his bed. In the middle of the pile was Scabbers. This was Christian's prized, three-inch stuffed rat he carried everywhere. The only problem was that Scabbers often got misplaced. But no matter how often he would go missing, Scabbers always showed up again. Stephen asked Christian why he'd packed Scabbers in his duffel bag. Christian replied,

"Because Scabbers always comes back and if you have Scabbers, you'll come back too."

Over the course of Stephen's final days in Afghanistan, Scabbers had many adventures. In addition to traveling to Egypt with another soldier and having his picture taken with the Pyramids in the background, Scabbers also got to hang from a helicopter and go into battle with Stephen and other soldiers who took him on loan to ensure they too would come back from some very scary places.

"Because Scabbers always comes back and if you have Scabbers, you'll come back too."

In June 2007, Stephen was injured in a Troops in Contact (TIC) where he tore his rotator cuff while trying to relocate a machine gun under heavy fire. It wasn't until the battle was over that he felt the pain and realized he couldn't lift his right arm. With only a couple of months before his tour was to end in August, he requested to be assessed at the Army hospital in Landstuhl, Germany rather than returning home for immediate treatment. This way, he could complete his tour with his unit. I flew to Germany to spend the week with him before he was sent back to Afghanistan. He wasn't even close to mended and would need surgery. At least he could help out by advising from a desk even if he did need help with his body armor when leaving the Forward Operating Base (FOB).

When he returned home, he had to have surgery on his rotator cuff and then nine months of physical therapy. This allowed him a lot of family time, which he needed to readjust to civilian life. The catch-22 with PTSD and the Army is they want their soldiers to get help, but once you raise your hand, your career is over. Hence Stephen, like so many other soldiers, suffered in silence. For most of that year, he was present physically, but mentally he was far, far away. I could tell from his blank express as he sat on the couch that he had closed himself off. This lasted for almost a year.

Stephen's experience in Afghanistan left him with an interesting take on priorities. When he would see others upset over normal daily life, his response was, "If nobody's dying, it's a good day." He just couldn't be bothered to amp out over what he now deemed as trivial, even though prior to Afghanistan he would have been just as upset as any other person over these mundane inconveniences. Little did I know that while I couldn't understand or relate to what he was experiencing at that time, in the near future, I would know all too well this same apathy for the trivial.

Shortly after Stephen's return, our neighbor stopped by one evening with her son. She explained that Christian, who was the same age as Jacob, had been picking fights and was bullying him. Stephen and I were both a bit shocked and saddened by the news. Stephen suspected he knew why this was happening and pulled Christian aside.

"Son, why do you think I went to Afghanistan?"

Christian responded, "To fight!"

"No, son, I went to Afghanistan to protect those who could not protect themselves. What you are doing to Jacob is exactly what I tried to stop."

Christian idolized his father and from that day forward never initiated a fight but was always the first to stand up and defend someone in need. Ironically, Jacob ended up becoming a close friend and was a pallbearer at Christian's funeral eleven years later.

When Christian turned eight years old, he joined Cub Scouts. I never appreciated the Boy Scout program until my son was a member. Although, I will admit, some of the activities put on by the Scout Master seemed a bit dangerous. "Hey, let's shoot these speeding water rockets into the air and let them free fall back to earth in the middle of the crowd. What could possibly go wrong?" Christian loved every part of it—the troop, the pinewood derby, fire building, and day camp.

It was just before his first day camp when I received notice that pocketknives would be on sale at the camp.

Before he left that morning, I gave him five dollars to spend at the Trading Post with specific instructions not to buy a knife. Later that day when Christian came home, I asked how he spent the money. He proudly pulled the knife from his pocket. In his excitement he had completely disregarded my instructions. This was typical Christian.

"Son, let's put this into our emergency supply kit," I bargained.

A few weeks later he asked, "Mom, when is there going to be an emergency so I can use my knife?"

"Hopefully never, son!" I responded.

At the age of 12 Christian moved from Cub Scouts into Boy Scouts. Stephen became the Scout Master and fast tracked all the boys in preparation for their Eagle. Christian enjoyed Scouts and being with his father. He was an expert with knots and camping. We always said if there was one person you wanted to be lost in the wilderness with, it was Christian.

Some of the funniest memories leaders would tell later were of Christian making his own comfortable hammock from rope, trying unsuccessfully to hike a mountain with an extra ten pounds of unnecessary weapons on his person, and always having to be scrutinized upon check- in because he had a knife hidden somewhere on his person.

Just before he turned 14, Christian completed all his requirements for his Eagle, which he received shortly after his birthday. It was a momentous day in our family with a huge celebration, including my sister who was a bird trainer, bringing an eagle to our ceremony.

Christian had quite a reputation among the neighborhood boys due to his interest in anything unsafe, flammable, or explosive. Some of his adventures over the years included setting off a rocket in my bedroom, creating a chemical explosion in the backyard that rocked our house, and making a homemade flamethrower which he was hooking up to a propane tank in the garage as I came driving in.

My neighbor, Tami, sent me the following text, "Hey, my boys just got a text from Christian asking them to come over to see his homemade dry ice bomb. Should I be concerned?"

"Yes, you should be very concerned. We should all be concerned!" I texted back. I barely made it to the backyard before it went off, burning his hand. This only served to increase his reputation among the boys for doing crazy things.

Every year in our Christmas letter to friends I would write, "We survived another year with Christian."

Chapter 4

SUICIDE FORESHADOWING

---

*I'll put a bullet in my head before I'll ever
lose my mind to Alzheimer's.*

~ LARRY DEAN

MY FATHER HAD LIVED IN OUR BASEMENT APARTMENT long
before Christian was born. My greatest fear was that one
of my children would find him with a bullet in his head.
My father's bipolarity usually manifested itself in spurts of
excitement and grand ideas, only to be followed by weeks
of depression and isolation. He would join us for family
gatherings, but often did not stay very long, even though
he wanted to be with us. His compulsion to isolate was
just too great.

His will to live waned over the years, and I became
especially concerned when he had DNR (Do Not Resus-
citate) tattooed on his chest. He also purchased an additional life insurance policy for accidental death, and he

My greatest fear was that one of my children would find him with a bullet in his head.

often engaged in some pretty extreme motorcycle riding. He spoke often of dying, which led me to believe he was considering suicide. While he did see a therapist off and on and took medication, it wasn't enough to save him in the end.

In November 2013, my father had knee surgery and stayed in a recovery facility before coming back home. He couldn't drive for the first few weeks and was going stir crazy, so I would occasionally pick him up and take him on an outing.

During this time, his bipolar medication was changed and became ineffectual. He wasn't sleeping very well, and he was in a lot of physical pain from his surgery. This lasted until January 15th when he was in a car accident. We believe he fell asleep and drifted into the back of a snowplow, which was parked at the side of the road.

Although he was hurt, this is not what killed him. A witness told the Highway Patrol that when he ran up to my dad's car, Dad pulled out a gun and started waving him away. The man retreated but heard a gunshot shortly thereafter. My father was taken to the hospital and put on life support. The DNR instructions obviously went unheeded.

About midday I received a call from my brother-in-law. "Lark, your father was in a serious car accident and is in critical condition. He's at the Intermountain Medical Center on life support. You need to go to the hospital right away because you're listed on his medical power of attorney."

"What? I'm on his medical power of attorney? When did that happen? Why didn't he prepare me?" I blurted out, still unable to process everything he was saying.

When I arrived at the hospital shortly thereafter, the doctor told me my father had sustained a gunshot wound to the head and would never fully recover even if he were able to function on his own without life support. My father and I had had enough conversations over the years that I knew he had no desire to live like this. I contacted my six siblings and waited for them to arrive over the next couple hours. Two were so far away, that they couldn't easily travel to us within a couple of hours, so they did not come.

Four of my six siblings, Skye, my mother, divorced from my dad for over 35 years by then, my former step-mother, who was a nurse in that very same hospital, and some close friends, were all gathered around my dad's hospital bed. My husband was out of town that day and tried to support me as best he could via the phone. Having been in Iraq when his mom was hospitalized and passed away a few years earlier, he knew how emotional this situation could be.

The final authorization to remove life support had to be given. Everyone turned to me as I stood at the end of the bed. I felt the weight of my decision as I gave the approval and the nurses turned off the life support and monitors, so we wouldn't know the exact time when he passed away.

We then said our goodbyes to my father and waited. Several of my sisters were distraught at the impending out-come. Turns out I was the right one to make this decision, and Dad probably knew it. Just like I would five years later with Christian's death, I functioned in purely task-mode when confronted with this. Emotions got put into a box to be dealt with later.

My relationship with my father had not been an easy one. I did not agree with several of his life choices nor did I feel very forgiving toward him for his lack of parental support. He was an emotionally distant parent and not very engaged in my life. I thought this would make his death easier, but I was wrong.

What followed was five months of deep, dark despair as I struggled to make sense of his death. I do not remember how my kids got fed or what I did during these months. As his executor, I would go to meetings, take notes, and then try to recall what had happened in the meeting. I don't remember much of that time.

The worst day was removing his personal effects from his totaled vehicle. All the rage and anger I had bottled up came pouring out in my sobs as the impending break down finally happened. Words cannot describe my frustration toward him for putting me in the situation of wiping off his gray matter to retrieve his files from the passenger seat. My thought was, "What parent puts their child in this situation?"

Looking back, I realize that despite the instability of my youth, my father provided me with several foundational pieces. First, because he had his master's degree, I knew I would get my master's. I never said it out loud, but I knew inside this was the goal. Second, my father encouraged me to take risks and follow my dreams—even when others didn't understand. Finally, his example taught me to question societal norms and discover what was true for me. I had permission to live my life my way.

Another significant outcome of my father's suicide was how it would later impact my son. While I didn't tell everyone exactly how my father died, I did tell my children. I felt it was important to be honest with them as they were bound to find out the truth at some point.

Statistics show that a suicide in the family increases the likelihood by fifty percent of another family member doing the same. The numbers were already stacked against my son with suicide being the number one killer of youth in Utah. Now his odds of dying this way just doubled with his grandfather's suicide. It suddenly became a viable option for Christian if life ever got too hard.

Chapter 5

TENUOUS TRUCE

Greater love hath no man than this,
that a man lay down his life for his friends.

~ JOHN 15:13 KJV

THE SUMMER OF 2015, RIGHT BEFORE CHRISTIAN entered
his sophomore year, is what I call the Beginning of the
End. One Sunday evening Stephen was having an actions/
consequences talk—something that Christian needed
every so often to get back on track. During this talk, Stephen noticed some signs of detachment on Christian's part.
Having been trained in the military to watch for signs of
suicide, Stephen asked, "Are you thinking of suicide?"

Looking down, Christian responded, "Yes."

Stephen immediately walked inside and told me,
"Christian is feeling suicidal. Please go talk with him. I'm
going to call the military suicide hotline and get him an
appointment with a therapist."

I will admit to feeling a bit odd about the situation. I didn't think Christian was saying this because he wanted attention. I just didn't think he would actually go through with killing himself. Even though I'd occasionally been in that dark hole where I didn't know if I would ever stop feeling pain, I had never taken the next step to actually come up with a plan to kill myself. I had also told my children how devastating my father's suicide had been for me. Surely this was enough to prevent them from walking down this path.

The next day I took Christian to see a therapist. She talked with him for almost an hour before having me come into the room where she asked, "Should I tell her, or do you want to?"

Christian peered at me closely and answered, "No, I'll tell her. Mom, I don't believe in God. I believe in science."

I think he was expecting me to blow up and start yelling. I simply replied calmly, "Okay, Son, I believe God is science, but you run with that if it makes you feel better. I can't make you believe anything. That's up to you."

Clearly, Christian had been feeling a lot of pressure to think or believe in a certain way, which did not resonate with him. The sad part is that he did not feel comfortable enough to have this conversation directly with either his father or me. The good part is that I accepted what he said without becoming angry.

Christian saw his therapist for about two months then told me, "Mom, I'm feeling better and don't need to go any more."

I never thought to ask him about his mental health after that. It just didn't occur to me that he could still be struggling, since outwardly he seemed fine. This lapse is one of my greatest regrets and was an oversight that foreshadowed his future suicide in ways I had no way of knowing.

As a parent I feel more strongly than ever that our role is to love and guide our children. Too often we think their actions will reflect poorly on us as parents or that calmly accepting them equates to our condoning their choices. This is not the case.

What if my son had said, "Mom, I'm gay," or "Mom, I got my girlfriend pregnant"? As parents we need to create a safe space where our children can talk with us openly without fear that we will cut them off or cast them out. I will admit to not feeling this way in my younger years of parenting, but now I feel strongly that this is the way to show our children unconditional love.

Christian was my most sensitive child. Possibly because he felt different, he was always ready to support his friends and loved ones. He would attend Gay Pride rallies because a couple of his friends were gay. He would help and watch over the older neighbors and developed a loving relationship with them. When his younger sister came to him crying because she dented his beloved Camaro, he hugged her and said, "That's okay, we can fix it."

> *As parents we need to create a safe space where our children can talk with us openly without fear that we will cut them off or cast them out.*

Christian's relationship with Stephen was mostly fun and stimulating. They were both into science and loved discussing chemical experiments or bouncing scientific theories off each other. Christian had a quick mind and could compute complex equations in his head or spout off one-liners that were hysterical. He was funny, quirky, and definitely danced to the beat of his own drum.

Christian was loving and kind to everyone but his mom. He looked at me as his jailer and killjoy. I looked at him as the disturber of my peace and order. In an attempt to minimize arguments at this time, I removed myself from micro-managing his school work and made it clear that he was responsible for his homework and grades, which would affect his ability to get into college and pursue the career he'd always wanted—mechanical engineering. After all, if Mom got amped out and worried over his grades, he didn't have to worry. Within a couple of weeks of my disengaging from his schoolwork, his slipping grades reversed and started to go back up. He realized I was serious about putting one hundred percent of the responsibility on him.

My frustration with Christian's blatant opposition to my role as parent played on my mind every day. His constant arguing with me about everything infuriated me. It was as if I represented all the restrictions that kept him from a life of fun and ease. "Yes, son, you do need to shower every day. You also need to wash your dirty laundry, take out the trash, and put the dishes away." His daily chores might have averaged ten minutes, yet you would think I had turned him into Cinderella from the way he fought me.

One day as I was walking down the hall, completely consumed with my rage over Christian's lack of support, a voice came into my head which said, "He's not the problem, you are." This brought me up short. No parent likes to be told they're doing it wrong, and I especially didn't want to hear it. How could I be the one at fault here?

A scene came into my mind of Christian and me talking in heaven before coming to earth. "Mom, you're going to have a lot of problems learning to be Christ-like, but I'm going to help you."

I immediately realized that because of my struggles with my son, I had to learn to take a softer approach in my interactions with him. I had to become less militant and demanding and become more understanding—as hard and as inadequate as my efforts were.

Christian's role in my life was a blessing, not a burden. This was especially evident after his suicide as I became kinder and more compassionate toward others. I was less apt to judge and quicker to lend support and understanding. My son's mission was to help me become more Christian—just like his name.

My son's mission was to help me become more Christian—just like his name.

As I look back, I wish I had worked harder to resolve the rift that started between us at an early age. I was so caught up in the day-to-day of my career, managing a household, and taking care of kids that I put relationships on the back burner, thinking they would sort themselves out at some point. As Christian got older, I just wanted him to stop arguing about everything I asked him to do. Consequently, I minimized the number of interactions I had with him, thinking that when he was out on his own, we might be able to have a better relationship. Our conversations were short and occurred only when necessary as we used mostly notes back and forth to communicate our wishes. "C, I have some people coming over so please tidy your study area including throwing away your trash. Love, Mom" or "Mom, we need more milk, C."

I made it through his last few years of high school feeling like I was serving a prison sentence and counting the days until he was out. While our older daughter, Skye, lived at home to attend a nearby college, I made it clear that Christian did not have this option. I felt depressed and frustrated with my boy who demeaned and disregarded my counsel as a parent. Whatever I said, he had to do the opposite. He made it clear with every conversation that I knew nothing.

As the spring of his senior year approached, I was practically giddy with joy. There was light at the end of the tunnel! I wanted him out on his own so he would finally appreciate all I had done for him. He could come home for Sunday dinner if he wanted, but that was it until he matured.

We were having the game room painted, so I boxed up his electronic equipment. I let him know it was packed and ready to go with him when he moved out at the end of the summer. This is when it hit him that I was completely serious about his leaving—whether he wanted to or not.

That summer he introduced me to Grace, his official

girlfriend. Their relationship seemed to soften him, and he began to be more polite toward me. He argued a bit less and started to tidy up a bit more. I softened and told him we might be able to work out a living situation that would allow him to stay at home while he attended college.

He had done a lot of concurrent enrollment classes and had a year of college completed by the time he graduated from high school. Since he was going into engineering, this meant he still had four years of schooling left, but at least he had his prerequisites out of the way, which usually added an additional year to those pursuing engineering. Could I survive four more years with Christian?

I agreed to start with the first semester as a trial period. He stepped up a little to what I asked of him, and I relaxed a little on my requirements. Neither of us was completely happy, but we were learning to get along.

In the spring of 2019, I had been learning about relationships—what real love is and what it is not. I realized I had been putting a lot of qualifiers on my children in order for them to have my love and approval. I decided to change my behavior. I met with each child separately and discussed my past parenting behavior and how I wanted to change in the future. I asked for feedback on what they would like to see different in our family. Because of these talks, my husband and I rescinded some of the family rules, giving the kids more autonomy. Keep in mind that our youngest was eighteen, but we still held a strong conviction that if you lived at home you followed our rules.

This dinner with my son happened two weeks before his death. After the waiter took our order, Christian asked me, "Mom, why did you and Dad force me to attend church? Why didn't you give me the choice, because maybe then I would have actually enjoyed going?"

"Son, you're probably right. Dad and I were doing the best we knew at the time. When you become a parent, I'm certain you'll make mistakes. However, you'll be doing the best you can with the knowledge you'll have at the time." Never would I have considered this future was soon to be beyond his reach.

I am so grateful I was able to create a safe space for Christian to express himself openly. We had a beautiful conversation with him doing most of the talking. He seemed happy and optimistic, but I don't think he shared all that was troubling him. At least we were able to converse without anger or blame. This was a great comfort to me after he passed away.

Chapter 6

I THINK YOU'RE MY DADDY

My FaceBook post January 31, 2018
WE'RE EXPECTING!

NOT QUITE IN THE TRADITIONAL WAY, but it's still an addition to the family!

Have you seen the movie *Elf* where Buddy learns about his true identity and travels from the North Pole to meet his cantankerous father who knows nothing about his existence? Well, our situation is a Buddy reincarnate except that his name is Caleb Thurman and he lives in Louisiana. The cantankerous father, Stephen Galley, is spot on though. Additionally, unlike the *Elf* story, Caleb has a lovely wife, Diana, and three girls plus a boy on the way. Poof! Instant grandparents. It's somewhat of a shock for all parties, but we are excited and happy to welcome them to our family!

Imagine our surprise to find out we're not only the parents of a 27-year-old son but also grandparents! Turns out Stephen left more behind in Louisiana than he realized. Unlike my first husband, Stephen did not cheat on me. He had a relationship with Caleb's mom, Brenda, long before we met. The circumstances were such that Caleb's parentage came into question, and DNA testing was not an economical option at the time. Stephen and Brenda ended up parting ways shortly after she became pregnant with no opportunity to reconnect. This was unfortunate because pictures of Caleb as a child clearly show his resemblance to Stephen. No DNA test required!

Caleb grew up thinking the man his mom was married to was his birth father. After his parents divorced, he never felt comfortable at his dad's house but didn't understand why. When he was eight he asked, "Mom, do I have to go to Dad's house?"

As a teenager, Caleb was estranged from the man he thought was his father. At 17, he learned some shocking news when he called Brenda from a tattoo parlor. "Mom, I want to get my last name tattooed on my back, but they won't do it without your permission since I'm underage."

"That might not be such a good idea, Caleb. You should come over. We need to talk."

Caleb drove over to her house where he found her crying at the kitchen table. She finally turned to her sister-in-law, Patricia, and said, "Tell him, I can't."

"He's not your father," said his aunt.

"I don't even care!" exclaimed Caleb, who had moved out and was used to living on his own. He got the tattoo anyway.

It wasn't until ten years later, when Diana was pregnant with his own son, that Caleb decided to solve the mystery of his paternity. He convinced his mom and older sister to accompany him to a lab which did DNA testing. His mom's DNA was identified and removed from the equation. The male DNA was then compared. The results clearly showed his father was not the same man as his sister's.

In the lobby, Brenda told Caleb, "Your biological father is Stephen Galley. I have no idea how to get in touch with him. All I remember is that he used to be in the military."

Without telling his mom, Caleb, Diana, and his brother-in-law, Joey, started the social media manhunt for Stephen. Caleb hadn't asked how to spell Stephen Galley, so they searched every possible name combination in hopes of finding Caleb's birth father. It was Joey who stumbled upon Stephen's Facebook profile, which showed him in uniform. He then pointed out a photo of Stephen as a teenager which looked very much like Caleb at the same age.

They were quite sure they had identified the correct man, but Caleb's attempts to connect with Stephen through Facebook went completely unanswered. Stephen's military background makes him fairly suspicious of everyone. Unless he knows you, he will not respond, and even then, it's not guaranteed.

After several unsuccessful attempts to connect with Stephen via Messenger, Caleb finally wrote directly on Stephen's Facebook wall, "Please contact me. It's important." He also listed his email and cell phone number in a very public place—not something you would normally do.

Finally, Stephen responded directly back on his wall, "What is this concerning?"

"It's a private matter." Caleb wrote back.

Stephen then switched over to Messenger where he wrote, "What do you want?"

It took Caleb a while to compose his thoughts before typing out, "I'm just going to come out and say it. My mother, Brenda, told me you were my father. I took a DNA test with my sister and found out the man I thought was my father is not a match. I would really like to meet my biological father."

Stephen's military interrogation skills kicked in and he simply responded, "I want to restate this to ensure I am getting it correctly. You took a DNA test and it did not match your father or sister, but your biological mother is Brenda. Is this correct?"

"Yes," typed Caleb.

They ended up meeting and agreeing to the DNA test, which came back as a ninety nine percent match. It was official. Both Stephen and his mother's example of unconditionally accepting Skye helped me do the same for Caleb and his family. Additionally, this experience turned out to be one of the greatest blessings in our life and would be instrumental in our healing process after Christian died.

When we broke the news to our kids, they too were shocked. Skye recovered first. As she was already out on her own, she had a more mature perspective. Christian and Victoria were stone-faced. I could see they were working through a lot of emotions. Christian had always wanted a brother, but after my clear declaration when he was nine that this was never going to happen, he stopped asking.

Now everything had changed. Not only was Christian no longer the only son, he was also not the oldest son. Where did that put my very alpha-male-conscious boy in the family hierarchy?

We had already planned a trip back to New Orleans in early February to visit Stephen's aunt and uncle, and we thought this would be a good time for us to meet Caleb and his family. Christian was already part of that trip, so he was the first child to meet his new sibling, sister-in-law, and three nieces. He immediately took to the girls and enjoyed his new role as uncle. When they came to Utah to visit us in November of that year, Christian was very inter-active with all the kids. He especially enjoyed

having a new nephew and snuggled him frequently on his shoulder.

Kayne was born the week following our initial visit. You would have thought Stephen was the one giving birth instead of Diana, he was so proud. Stephen walked around the entire day with a smile so big you couldn't wipe it from his face. His first grandson. I could see his plans for hunting, fishing, and camping already taking shape.

My relationship with Caleb brought to light some interesting observations. First, I never wanted his birth mom to feel slighted or marginalized by our coming into Caleb's life after all the hard work of raising him had been done. Second, I did not like the word "stepmom" and its negative connotations. Before even meeting Caleb, I sent him a message, requesting he address me as "Bonus Mom." He later told me he never thought such a strange title would stick, but after meeting his friends, coworkers, and family, they all easily referred to me as "Bonus" Mom, which we found hilarious. By the way, I refer to Caleb as "Bonus Boy."

Could I not release these and love and accept him for the person he was?

Something else I realized about my relationship with Caleb was that it came with no baggage. I did not have a history of arguing and fighting as I did with Christian. It was actually easier for me to accept and love Caleb than it was for me to accept and love Christian. How could I harbor such animosity toward him? I began to see that my anger toward Christian was due to a buildup of expectations and criticism for his choices. Could I not release

these and love and accept him for the person he was—exactly how I loved and accepted Caleb?

In retrospect, I see God's timing in this event. Caleb and his family came into our lives just over a year before Christian died. It gave them enough time to get to know Christian and feel his personality. It also allowed us the time to create a strong enough bond that on the day Christian passed away, Stephen cried out, "I need Caleb here!" Not as a replacement son but as a strength and support to our family when we were so very devastated.

Stephen and Christian enjoyed talking about chemical combinations and complex math equations. Stephen and Caleb enjoy talking about LSU football and Southern cooking methods. They are two different sons with their own unique ways of bonding with their father.

The grandchildren also played a role in 'our healing, especially for Stephen. The girls all thought he walked on water because he would give them whatever they wanted and the grandson's pronunciation of papa as "poppit" only made him more endearing. Knowing there were little people in the world who loved him so fiercely gave Stephen some hope for the future.

The holidays that first year were especially hard. We found a lot of solace in spending time together. The entire extended family spent the week after Thanksgiving at Disney World. The four of us also flew out to Louisiana to spend the week of Christmas with Caleb and family. On the way home, Skye told me she felt like she had always known Caleb, he was so integrated into our family.

I know Victoria felt the same because she mercilessly tormented her older brother like all good little sisters should. God's timing in bringing this family into our lives was a tender mercy and evidence that there is beauty even in the pain.

Chapter 7

THE DAY OUR WORLD ENDED

O my son Absalom, my son, my son Absalom! Would God I had died for thee, O Absalom, my son, my son!

~ SAMUEL 18:33 KJV

THE IRONY OF SUICIDE IS THAT EVEN THOUGH PEOPLE feel worse during the winter months, the majority don't take their life until spring when they start to feel better. In retrospect, I think Christian had a plan in the back of his mind, and when things got too hard, he had already decided he was going to be "done."

Three events happened within the same time frame that triggered his suicide. As adults, we can look at life and think, "While this is not great, it will pass." A teenager with limited life perspective can't see past tomorrow, let alone a few

> *In retrospect, I think Christian had a plan in the back of his mind, and when things got too hard, he had already decided he was going to be "done."*

months down the road. Life got overwhelming. He lost hope and impulsively followed through on his suicide plan without realizing the impact of his actions.

The week before Christian died, he'd been in a car accident. There had been some snow on the road, and he was traveling a bit too close. The driver in front of him slammed on his brakes to avoid hitting the car in front of him. Christian was unable to stop in time and crashed, almost totaling his own car.

Christian needed to pay the deductible, which he could cover with his savings, but he also needed transportation to and from school while his car was in the shop. He'd been using his dad's second car, but Stephen wanted Christian to call the insurance company to see if our policy covered a loaner in this instance. It was a bit of tough love as we'd been forcing Christian to take the lead with the insurance company, which he'd not been doing very well.

Another issue Christian was dealing with was slipping grades. It was his second semester in engineering and the material was getting harder. He had been masking this by joking and avoiding his father's questions about school. In retrospect, I can see that the two weeks prior to his suicide were actually marked by more erratic behavior than usual. Christian would tease and wrestle with his father, which was usual, but he'd taken it up a notch to where he was bordering on physically hurting his dad.

On the evening of March 20, 2019, my husband and I went to bed at 10 p.m. I fall asleep quickly, but my husband has had sleeping issues since he returned from

Afghanistan. At 11 p.m., Christian returned from school, as was his pattern since he usually stayed in the lab to get as much tutoring as possible. For some reason, Stephen thought this would be an excellent time for a parental chat just like the one he'd had back when Christian was entering his Sophomore year in high school. While nothing he said was out of line, I don't think any good comes of late-night showdowns.

"Christian, you need to understand that your latest ticket, along with your two prior speeding tickets, is probably going to get your license suspended. You're going to need to come up with some alternative transportation to and from school if this happens." The week following Christian's death we received a letter from the DMV revoking his license for a month, just as we suspected would happen.

Stephen continued, "You've also been avoiding answering me about your grades. I want a straight, honest answer about what they are."

"This semester has been getting a lot harder, and I'm not doing well. My grades have dropped to B's and C's," answered Christian.

Since we contribute to tuition based on performance, lower grades meant he was going to need to come up with a lot more money toward fall tuition. "You're going to need to earn some money to cover fall tuition, but you can work for me over the summer to earn it," Stephen told him. "You also need to know that I've mapped out your classes for the next three years, and school is only going to get harder. The reason I'm telling you all this is I love you. Most parents wouldn't take the time to explain this to their kids."

Hearing all this after a long day at school, and knowing the pressure to perform was only going to get harder, seemed to overwhelm Christian. He must have felt he had disappointed his father, who was his best friend. I don't think anything my husband said was out of line. It was just poor timing after a long day at school and the worries about his car and tuition. My husband went to bed that night. My son did not.

The next morning, I awoke and left early to teach a class. Before leaving I remembered two things. First, my husband alluded to his talk with Christian the night before. Second, I noticed the hand wash had been put away and the garbage taken out—two chores over which Christian argued incessantly. My thought as I left the house was, "Thank you, Son, for taking care of your jobs!" I learned later that many suicide victims make sure all their tasks are completed before following through with their death. It's as if they're saying, "All tidied up. I can go now."

Here is where we come to my heart-stopping moment on Thursday, March 21, 2019 at 10 a.m. when the police officer entered the building. Was he here for one of the actual occupants of the building or maybe there was a parking issue with a training attendee? Even when he asked to take me to a back office to speak privately, I was still not alarmed.

As I looked up at the kind officer, I could tell he was heavy with some bad news. "I'm sorry to inform you that your son is dead."

I didn't respond. My mind went into denial and my heart closed. I displayed no emotion. This was not possible. I had seen Christian just the day before. Things like this didn't happen to real people. I thought back to his accident the week before and asked, "Was it a car accident?"

"No. He shot himself at home," the officer answered.

Still I displayed no emotion. My mind raced to find a different interpretation of what he was saying. Suicide— the intentional taking one's life? That was even worse than a car accident which offered some passivity and possible transfer of responsibility. Suicide spoke of a dark, empty hole that my husband and I were not even aware existed for our son.

I finally blurted out, "I'm sorry to appear so detached, but I'm in denial. I don't understand and cannot believe it's possible."

The officer kindly asked me, "Can you drive? Do you want to ride with me? We need you to come home right away."

> *Suicide spoke of a dark, empty hole that my husband and I were not even aware existed for our son.*

Here's where Ice Queen kicked in and my ability to completely isolate and compartmentalize my emotions took over. I had an obligation to the people who had traveled up to an hour to attend my class. I couldn't change anything at home. I would stick this horrible event—which clearly was a mistake—in the back compartment of my mind, lock the door, and deal with it later.

"I can drive. I have to finish my class and can be home in two hours."

The police officer could tell he was not getting through to me. "Your husband *needs* you at home. You need to come home now."

Still in complete denial I said, "Give me ten minutes to work with my co-host and I'll leave."

Looking back, I'm sure the officer thought I was a terrible wife and mother. What human on this planet is so detached and cold? It wasn't until several days later that I understood exactly why I had acted this way.

Back in 2006 right before my husband left for Afghanistan, we watched the movie *We Were Soldiers,* which tells of a group of men who fought in Vietnam. They left their wives behind on base. When the men started dying, two uniformed Department of Defense men would show up on the doorstep and break the news to the wife, who would immediately break into hysterics. I felt that was going to happen to my husband. He was going to Afghanistan and wouldn't come back.

I decided that when someone in a uniform comes to tell me of his death, I would be ready. I would not break down wailing and falling apart. Never did I suspect this decision, which was lodged in the back of my mind, would kick in and take over when a uniformed policeman showed up to tell me about my son's death.

It was as if I was going through the motions of a prede-termined scene. I escorted the policeman to the front door of the office and asked my mother, who was in the class, to step outside. She already knew something was wrong before I told her about Christian.

"Mom, Christian has shot himself and is dead. I need to go home. Would you please help my co-trainer with the class then tidy up the room and come to my house?"

With sadness in her eyes, she patted my hand and said, "Sure."

I did not tell the attendees what had happened but merely said, "There's been a family emergency, and I need to leave."

As I got into my car, I checked my phone. There were several texts from neighbors.

"Lark, I see the ambulance and fire truck in front of your house. Is there anything I can do to help?"

"Lark, why are the police at your house? What can I do for you?" They knew something was wrong long before I did.

I calmly drove home to face reality. Still there were no tears. These wouldn't come for another week as I held my emotions in check and carried the rest of the family through our private hell.

I arrived home to a relatively quiet house. My friend and neighbor, Julie Erwin, was there. She was the one Ste-phen called right after calling the police. She had come over and was instrumental in coordinating things with the police, EMTs, and the medical examiner's office.

My husband was disconsolate as he held me and sobbed. "It's my fault. It's all my fault. I am so, so sorry."

"Stephen, it was not your fault. I'm certain there were many factors in Christian's choice and no one thing was the reason for his death. We didn't know what had happened earlier in the day or whether he might have chosen suicide in a month or a year from now. He made the decision to end his life."

Earlier that morning when Stephen hadn't heard our son getting ready for school, he called Christian's cell phone. It went immediately to voicemail. That was odd and he started to get a little worried. He shouted up the stairs for Christian to respond. Nothing. This increased his anxiety. He then climbed the stairs and found Christian's door locked. Still there was no sound from the other side.

That's when Stephen started to panic and rattled the door to shake the lock loose. He burst into the room and found his worst nightmare before his eyes. In his distress, he threw himself on Christian, sobbing.

The PTSD he'd experienced from Afghanistan kicked back in and two days later he was hallucinating as he tried to wipe the nonexistent blood from our bathroom sink saying, "There's so much blood. There's so much blood. I've got to clean up the blood."

I gently took his hands and said, "There's no blood here."

Stephen stopped eating and within a week had dropped fifteen pounds. Within a month he'd lost thirty pounds. It was all I could do to get him to eat at least five hundred calories a day. He seemed to want to waste away and disappear.

After finding Christian, Stephen called 911. He was barely coherent as he choked out, "My son is dead. He shot himself." Later we learned that Christian had used pillows to muffle the sound of the gunshot. This was why we had heard nothing in the night.

The police immediately responded and started their investigation. We were all suspects until they could determine the actual cause of death. My husband had disturbed Christian's body, which they didn't like. While logically Stephen knew not to do this, his emotions took over and he'd been unable to stop himself. The police quickly eliminated Stephen as a suspect as his overwhelming grief made it very evident he could not have done this. There was also a note from my son which clearly spelled out that he had intended to take his life.

When I returned home, Christian's body was still upstairs where Stephen had found him earlier. I did not want to see him that way as the scene would have played out over and over in my mind. I wanted to remember Christian as he had been. Stephen also did not want me there when the medical examiner showed up to remove Christian's body. Someone needed to tell our youngest daughter, Victoria, who was a senior, what had happened. I headed over to the high school to tell her and be out of the way when the M.E. arrived.

When the police notified the high school of Christian's death, a counselor pulled Victoria from class on some pretext about graduation requirements. They did not want her to find out about her brother from a text or social media and asked as she came into the office, "Hello, Victoria. Why don't you put all your personal belongings under your chair while we talk?"

I was escorted by a school police officer to the counselor's office, where I found our happy Victoria laughing with the counselors. It was to be her last carefree moment for a long time. "Hi, Mom. What are you doing here?" she asked with a smile on her face.

"Hi, honey, I need to talk with you."

The police officer escorted us to a private room where he asked me quietly, "Do you want to tell her or should I?"

"No, I'll do it."

He waited outside while Victoria and I entered, closed the door, and sat down opposite each other. "I have something very hard to tell you. Christian shot himself at home and is dead." She let out a scream and started to sob and shake. "So this was how a normal person reacts to bad news," I thought.

We stayed in the room for several minutes while I held her. She then got a determined look on her face and said, "I have to run." She was on the cross country and track teams and was used to running four to nine miles a day. I wanted her to come home, but I also wanted to allow her the space to grieve in private as she and Christian were very close.

"Victoria, I will let you run, but you need to promise me that you are well and will not do anything to harm yourself. If you are unable to drive yourself home, call me and I will come back to get you."

"Okay," she said tersely.

I left her at school, but I will admit I was worried about her mental state and prayed I wouldn't lose two children that day.

I returned home without Victoria and called my older daughter, Skye, who was at work twenty minutes away. I calmly said, "There's been a family emergency. You need to leave work and head to the house right away. Dad and I are okay, but you need to come home now."

"All right, I'll head out in five minutes. Just let me collect my things," she said.

When Skye walked in the door, I hugged her and said, "Thank you for coming. Something very tragic has happened." She then saw her father in the living room. His face was pale and his eyes bright red and puffy. She immediately felt the weight of the situation and became very frightened as Stephen locked eyes and moved hastily toward her. He gripped her face and said, "I love you so much."

They sat down on the couch. I chose the ottoman opposite and held onto Skye's hand as I told her, "Christian shot himself and is dead." She too started to shake and sob. Once again, my reaction to his death felt completely abnormal. What was wrong with me that I could not show emotion at that level?

Skye drove to her home a while later to collect her personal items so she could stay with us for a few days. We

I will admit I was worried about her mental state and prayed I wouldn't lose two children that day.

all felt the urgent need to hold tightly to one another. She later told me, "I knew something was very wrong when you called, but it never occurred to me it could be a family calamity of this magnitude."

The rest of the day was laden with grief as we dealt with the bio crew who came after Christian's body had been taken away. This is the team who cleans up after horrific scenes like ours. They removed all the bedding, wiped the walls, and cut out a huge section of the carpet which I had a hard time forcing myself to replace until months later.

Stephen told them, "Get rid of everything on that side of the room."

One of the bio guys called out, "The bed is still completely intact and looks fine. Are you sure you want us to take it?"

"Yes, take that too." He remembered my experience with wiping down my dad's car and didn't want me to have a chance to repeat it with Christian.

I was also the one who sent out and responded to dozens of texts to family and friends. Stephen was completely incapable of functioning. I was barely functioning but managed to text a few words to those who needed to know. I often only responded with a heart emoji to people's texts or a brief text to their voice messages. I could not bring myself to actually speak to many people on the phone. Caleb was one of the few people I called. How do you tell a new son that a brother he'd met only the year before and was just getting to know had taken his life?

We asked our church leaders to request limited contact from our neighbors and congregation as it was so emotionally overwhelming to repeat the story over and over. People wanted to bring in meals, which we adamantly resisted at first, but soon relented due to the outpouring of kindness. It was a good thing too, as we stopped making any kind of meals and would have simply reverted to an occasional piece of toast. We had little appetite and no energy at all for the extraneous.

In the evening, a good friend and leader in our congregation, David Wahlquist, came by to give us words of comfort through a Priesthood blessing. When it was my turn, he spoke kind things to buoy me up but stopped in the middle and said slowly, "Lark, you have a lot of work to do. A lot of work to do." I couldn't help but think to myself, "My son just died today and you're talking to me about work? Isn't that somewhat inappropriate?" I fretted for days over what he meant and repeatedly asked myself, "What work?"

That night we all went to bed, but no one was sleeping. Skye, Stephen, and I roamed the house and eventually all ended up in Christian's room, even though half of it was stripped and bare. We spent several hours sitting on his floor and would occasionally say something to each other. More than anything we just wanted to be together and close to Christian. It was a long night mixed with so many regrets and conflicting emotions.

I seemed to have moved past the first stage of grief—denial—and was now onto stage two— anger. I was angry with Christian for causing this pain that was engulfing our family. I was angry for his shortsightedness in handling his problems, for devastating his father, and for placing such a heavy burden on my shoulders. Still I could not cry.

I reflected on my sister's experience a couple of years earlier. She'd been in a work meeting and felt prompted to leave right then and return home. Her colleagues were a bit upset and put out with her, but she was insistent and rushed home where she found her teenage son about to put a gun to his head. Why hadn't I been warned? Why hadn't someone intervened on my son's behalf? Was I not worthy of such a prompting? Where was my angel of mercy?

The next morning, we had an appointment with the funeral home and made decisions no parent is prepared to make. Stephen was a shell of himself, and we were grateful for the girls' help. They took over the decision on the flowers. Skye gathered all the pictures to turn into the funeral home, who would make a video for the viewing. I took on the task of writing the obituary.

We chose a guest sign-in book with an eagle on the cover to commemorate Christian's being an Eagle Scout. We picked out a beautiful casket that had to be all wood due to its final resting place being the family tomb in New Orleans, where Stephen's parents and grandparents had been interred. We were all so sad and disconsolate as we played our parts in this living nightmare.

The viewing would be one week away on a Friday evening with the first funeral being the following day and the second viewing and funeral being one week from Saturday in New Orleans. Having two funerals certainly stretched out our emotions and made it twice as hard, but it needed to be done for the sake of Stephen's family and friends in Louisiana. We were so grateful for the help of Stephen's sister, Hope Soto, who made all the arrangements with the New Orleans funeral home for the obituary, viewing, funeral service, and entombment.

Another odd memory during this time was our belief that we would never laugh again or that if we did it would be a betrayal to our son.

Another odd memory during this time was our belief that we would never laugh again or that if we did, it would be a betrayal to our son. Shouldn't we walk around in mourning and be forever sad now that he was gone? When we occasionally laughed about some memory, the reminder of his absence only seemed to engulf us more. It felt wrong to act normal or find happiness again.

Chapter 8

THE DECISION

---

*. . . who knoweth whether thou art come to the
kingdom for such a time as this?*

~ ESTHER 4:14 (KJV)

ON SATURDAY, TWO DAYS AFTER CHRISTIAN'S DEATH, I
started to feel myself sliding into the black hole where I
had spent five months after my father's suicide. Very few
people—even many of my best friends—didn't know my
father had died by suicide. The shame and stigma were too
great for me to face, and because I wouldn't talk about it, I
couldn't heal.

During those first five months after my father's death, I
mentally lost myself. I don't remember how my children got
fed or how I made it through daily tasks like showering and
eating. I do remember going to meetings, taking notes, and
then two days later looking at my notes, knowing it was my
handwriting but not remembering being in the meeting or

what the notes meant.

This total lack of mental clarity was scary and unfamiliar to me, so when I started to feel it creep in again, I became very afraid. I didn't want to lose five months or five years to this darkness. I needed to be present for my family or how would any of them survive? I simply did not have the luxury of disappearing.

Another reason for the dark hole was the whispering that I was a terrible mom and that Christian hated me. In his suicide note he had written, "Mom, love a little more and care a little less. It's more important to love someone for who they are than to waste their life wishing they were something they weren't. Time is short. Make the most of it now." I thought about his words over and over again and concluded it was *because* I loved that I cared so much about his wellbeing and choices.

While it would have been easier to allow Christian to ignore the long-term consequences of his choices, I was willing to show up for him every day because I cared. Skye reminded me that I had always read books and taken classes in the hopes of improving my relationship with him. Even in December, just three months earlier, I was getting one-on-one coaching in order to make it through the holidays with him. Also, I had just finished reading a parenting book a few weeks before his death that allowed me to create a safe space for us to have our dinner talk. I had not given up on this difficult child and for that I am grateful.

Still, the circumstances of his passing weighed on me, and I mentioned it to a coach whose mentoring group I had joined the month prior to Christian's death. "That's surprising," she said. "Another member of our group has the gift to speak with those who have passed and told me she had a beautiful conversation with your son."

I had to know what was said, so I called her, somewhat hesitant and skeptical. Since this person doesn't like to talk openly of her gift, I'll refer to her as Pam.

Pam told me, "I was so concerned when I saw your post in our private group that I began to wonder about his frame of mind and slipped into a meditative state. I saw him dressed in a dark gray suit flying on a trapeze in a huge empty space. There were several others doing the same thing, but they were far off and in their own space. Christian had a look of wonder on his face as he performed flips and acrobatics. (I can totally picture my son doing this.)

Pam continued, "As soon as he saw me, he jumped off the trapeze and ran to a Plexiglas barrier that separated us. He put his hand to the Plexiglas and said, "Tell my mom that I love her and that everything is going to be okay." Those were the exact words I needed to hear to heal my troubled heart. I knew he had forgiven me for my weakness, and I began to feel life might offer some meaning after all.

"Tell my mom that I love her and that everything is going to be okay."

Even more amazing is that this message of "Tell my mom that I love her" was repeated two more times that week. The last message came from my aunt who told me, "I have a message from Christian. He came to me during the last prayer of his funeral service and said, "Tell my mom that I love her and that I finally understand."

The second part of this message had specific meaning to me because I would often say to myself after an argument with him, "One day you will finally understand how painful your words and actions have been toward me." My words stem from my belief that we will all stand before God one day to answer for our actions. I never considered his time would be years before my own. His words let me know that he finally understood the reasons behind my actions and how very much I tried to love and parent him in a way that would help him.

In that same conversation, my aunt told me, "Christian also has a message for Stephen. He said to tell my dad that I love him, and I am so sorry. He was my best friend. I never meant to hurt him." These words were a salve to our grieving hearts.

I later asked a friend who had also lost a child why Christian could not have given these messages directly to me instead of through others. She told me, "Because you would have questioned it. Hearing the same message from three people allowed you to have no doubt that it was from him." I knew she was right.

In addition to the messages from my son, I also received several calls from my friends who had teenagers who knew Christian. They spoke of their grief, worry, and fear that their child, who was experiencing severe emotional turmoil, might make the same choice as my son.

I began to see that this event was not about what kind of parent I was and how I had failed to see the warning signs which might have allowed us to prevent his death. It was not about my son's mental anguish and his choice to kill himself. It wasn't even about whether or not these other children chose to take their own lives. I could not change or do anything about that. However, what I did have absolute control over was my ability to speak out about the situation. If one of these children ended their life because I chose not to speak out, that's where I would have failed. The risk to stay silent greatly outweighed the risk of speaking out.

On Tuesday, only six days after my son's passing, I was finally ready to tell the world how he had died. I made a decision that, while I could not change the past, I would do all in my power to change the future. I would find meaning in this tragedy and a reason to move forward in life rather than choosing to shrink back. The dark hole started to recede, and my very rocky journey began. It didn't make the loss easier, but it did make it more manageable. Sharing my message of value and hope became my reason for getting out of bed.

I finally knew what our church leader, David, meant when he said I had a lot of work to do. I took it as a literal calling from God and told Him, "I am not an expert in this field. I'm not a trained medical doctor, a licensed therapist, or even a counselor. I am just a concerned parent who wants desperately to prevent one other parent from experiencing what we have gone through. I will do whatever I can, but you, God, will have to open the way."

After Christian's death, I began to learn as much as

possible about suicide. I found out it was the number one killer of our youth in Utah and the tenth overall killer nationwide. I discovered males were three times as likely to be successful in their suicide attempts because their methods were more violent than those of females. I also learned the preferred term is "died by suicide," not "committed suicide," which connotes a crime has been committed. Finally, I learned I was referred to as a "suicide survivor" which is so ironic because I didn't feel like I was "surviving" anything.

I learned I was referred to as a "suicide survivor" which is so ironic because I didn't feel like I was "surviving" anything.

I started talking to everyone around me and posting on social media about this rampant epidemic. I considered it my personal mission to wake up every complacent parent who, like me, thought suicide was "out there" and not something that would ever impact my family. I shared the raw and hard stuff, which created a safe place for those who were hurting to share with me.

I was shocked at the people who came forward to tell me they had either attempted or were contemplating suicide. These did not appear to be "broken" people. Could the belief that one was not good enough be more pervasive than ever imagined?

A therapist told me, "Depressed people often start feeling better, not because they've turned a corner and are actually doing better, but because they've decided on a plan to end their life and know their 'out' is available when needed."

"That's what happened with my son! He's had his plan in place for the past three years. He wasn't better after those talks with his therapist. He was just biding his time until things would become too difficult to bear." Not knowing my son had lived in this state for so long was the most heartbreaking regret of my life.

The most amazing part of my journey was that sharing my story and grief over both my son's and father's suicides allowed me to start healing. This willingness to confront reality and say, "Yes, they died by suicide, but it's not the end!" gave me a reason bigger than myself to carry on with life. If you had told me before my son's death that I would be preaching from my soapbox about suicide prevention and even throwing in some references to God, I would have told you, "No way!" That is too scary and unimaginable, and yet that is exactly what I've been doing.

My decision to make something good come from a terrible situation allowed me to stand in strength at Christian's viewing a week after he had passed away. I was able to hold and comfort the many parents who showed up to grieve with us. I felt them shaking to their very core as they sobbed and knew they were as much concerned for their children as they were for mine.

> *My decision to make something good come from a terrible situation allowed me to stand in strength . . .*

We had some beautiful experiences at Christian's viewing and funeral. My friend, Leslee, had told me earlier, "Be on the lookout for signs from your son." I saw the first sign as I entered the funeral home prior to the viewing. The skies had just cleared after a light rain shower leaving behind a beautiful rainbow. This was a sign within our family as we often talked about the fire rainbow we saw at my mother-in-law's funeral nine years earlier. Several months later, I was to see the largest and most brilliant rainbow of my life as I drove home from a grieving mothers' retreat. I knew Christian was present during both these times and felt his desire for me to know he loved me.

Additionally, several of my family members spotted a large eagle flying over the church on the morning of the funeral. That same eagle was spotted a few days after the funeral, perched on our rooftop as Stephen and Victoria came driving home. We live in a fairly populated area, and I have never seen an eagle in the vicinity. We could only conclude that once again, Christian was nearby.

The third sign, which came within two weeks of his passing, was the jazz band playing in the French Quarter as we strolled along the afternoon of Christian's final funeral and interment in the family tomb. We all knew he would have loved this type of celebration as his memorial and had even talked about it the week prior. Once again, we felt him close.

At the first viewing, we met many of Christian's friends. Not only were there former high school friends, but his former principal, vice principal, and multiple teachers attended. His homeroom teacher, Mr. Lindsey, with whom I'd had several parent-teacher visits, told me, "I've seen many students who manifested signs of a troubled home life. I never noticed any of these signs in Christian." I was grateful to know we hadn't blatantly missed something that could have saved our son.

Several of Christian's fellow U of U students showed up. I'll always remember one young man in particular who stood weeping, too overwhelmed to speak. Another friend spoke up and told us he was from Illinois and had just moved out for the school year. Christian had spoken with him and taken him under his wing. The young man finally sobbed, "He was my first friend here."

We also learned that Christian had stayed late at the labs nightly, not so much for himself but to help his fellow students and friends understand the complex math and science material they were being taught. Both stories touched me as examples of his willingness to reach out and serve even in the smallest places.

Another insight we had about Christian was from his friends who played the card game Magic with him. Every Thursday and Friday night, Christian would show up at the game store to play Magic. It was an obsession with him, and he had amassed thousands of dollars in playing cards. He had even won a state-wide competition six months earlier and traveled to Denver to play at the national level. The workers from the store told us how much they liked Christian and that he was the only non-employee ever allowed behind the counter to occasionally help out.

The two youths whose mothers I had spoken with shortly after Christian's death also came through the line. Because of our talk, I knew they were struggling with suicide ideation.

My husband and I gave each of them an engulfing hug and pleaded, "If you are ever struggling, please get help from your parents if you feel depressed." They felt our overwhelming love and concern. They saw the devastating effects of the suicide on our family and realized they did not want their families to experience the same. Their mothers each told me later, "My child promised to never consider suicide again. Thank you." Two lives saved and grief averted from some very dear friends of ours.

The next day the church was packed near capacity for his funeral. There were hundreds of people who attended, many of them young adults. I thought of all the people Christian had impacted and realized we often have no idea how far-reaching our influence can be. Our friend, Rick, who spoke at the funeral, shared the story of Scabbers and how Christian had sent him off to Afghanistan to ensure his dad found his way home safely. Later the next week, before the interment, Stephen lovingly placed Scabbers in the coffin with Christian to ensure he would find his way home safely.

Over this past year I have seen God's hand in my life as I have tried to share my message of value and hope. He has opened doors, providing me with multiple opportunities to speak, as well as helping me write this book.

Stephen lovingly placed Scabbers in the coffin with Christian to ensure he would find his way home safely.

A good friend and one of my pre-readers commented, "I've known you for several years now and expected your book to be good. However, I did not expect it would be this good."

I agree. Sometimes I read passages of the book and realize it's not just me writing. I know I've had divine assistance to share what was in my heart.

Chapter 9

GRIEF AND THE
AFTERMATH OF LOSS

There were a million things I wanted to say to you.
Goodbye was not one of them.

~ ZOE CLARK-COATES

MY MISSION TO SPREAD THE MESSAGE of suicide prevention, personal value, and hope has been an emotional roller coaster. The beginning months were difficult, but they were filled with purpose. I believed the saying "time heals all wounds," and thought the grief would diminish with time. I was wrong.

Four and a half months after Christian's death, I wanted to shut down. My husband felt the same. We chose to stay home as much as possible and rarely left the house for anything other than work or groceries. Friends tried to get us to come out with them, but we didn't have it in us to socialize or discuss the trivial.

Skye said it best when a friend asked her, "What's so difficult about losing your brother?"

"Everything," she responded.

I liken it to moving through Jell-O. It completely engulfs you, making your movements slow and breathing almost impossible. It is a constant knowing that nothing will ever be the same again.

As time passed, the grief became a weight crushing down on my heart and shoulders. I could barely breathe. I pretended to function, but I couldn't get much done to help others when I felt so depressed.

As I discussed how I felt with a friend who does energy work, she said, "This isn't surprising since grief is stored in our lungs." That would certainly explain why every breath felt like a shearing pain inside my lungs and throat. Could I learn to breathe again without the pain?

She mentioned how grief is stored in our lungs. That would certainly explain why every breath felt like a shearing pain inside my lungs and throat. Could I learn to breathe again without the pain?

On the six-month anniversary of his death, I was attending a women's retreat in Southern Utah. The 21st of each month had always been hard, but this milestone felt especially heavy. As I walked alone, surrounded by the beautiful red rock, I pleaded with God and Christian to take away the burden of my pain. Not to take away the memories or even the sadness—just the part that made it difficult to function throughout the day. Immediately the heaviness was gone, and it has never returned. I still feel waves of loss and regret, but it is not the debilitating grief I had been experiencing. This is how I can carry on with spreading my message. I have been given divine support to allow me to comfort others, and I am grateful.

While the death of my son has been traumatic, it's the after-effects that have been so devastating to our family. The paralyzing grief has been unimaginable. Each person who knew Christian is having his or her own grief experience, based on the closeness of the relationship, past experiences, and their willingness to move forward. There were times when I felt that not only had I lost my son, I had also lost the rest of my family, as we each pulled away and turned inward to heal.

For my husband, Christian's suicide has been the worst experience of his life. Worse than his father wasting away for two years from cancer, worse than his mother dying somewhat unexpectedly from esophageal cancer, worse than making decisions that affected the lives of his soldiers, and worse than the undiagnosed PTSD that followed him home from Afghanistan. Not only was their relationship very close, Stephen was also the one who found Christian after his death. This in itself has been extremely traumatic, as Stephen too experienced being sucked down that dark hole of depression.

> *There were times when I felt that not only had I lost my son, but I had also lost the rest of my family, as we each pulled away and went inward to heal.*

After the initial shock of Christian's death passed, Stephen spent several hours each week working in the yard. This was not something he usually did. He probably spent more time digging up and replacing struggling trees and plants over the next six months than he ever did in the entire time we've lived in this house. Our good friend, Tonya Huntsman, gave us a "Christian tree," which he lovingly planted in a special place in our backyard. Gardening seemed to be somewhat healing for him.

Another change that took place was Stephen's lack of interest in the military. He served for 35 years, first in the Air Force, then Army National Guard, and most recently the Army Reserves. He earned several commendations including a Bronze Star for his service in Afghanistan. He also held several important positions, including his recent service as the Deputy Commander of North America for Defense Support of Civil Authorities. Suddenly, he was no longer able to continue as if everything was the same. His heart was just not able to bear it, so he retired.

Unlike my husband, this experience has not been the most debilitating of my life. My relationship with my son before his death was one of frustration. I remember being so angry with Christian that I could not cry for almost a week after his death. It was only when I saw the picture of him at six years old, holding Scabbers, that I finally broke down and sobbed over the loss of my sweet little boy.

I had also experienced the death of a marriage and the suicide of my father, which were both highly traumatic. Because I was personally familiar with that same dark hole of depression which both these experiences brought on, I made a conscious choice not to go there again. My son's death is not what I would have wanted, but I cannot change it. I can only change my perspective and choose to make something good out of something horrifying. It's those who refuse to accept reality and try to change what cannot be changed who are stuck in their grief.

What helped me continue to live one more day was my desire to help others, being alert to the signs which showed me Christian was nearby, and feeling an overwhelming sense of joy when I shared his story of hope. Also comforting was hearing his specific words, which had special meaning to me and were exactly what I needed to hear. I knew these were from him and not made up by someone else.

> *It's those who refuse to accept reality and try to change what cannot be changed who are stuck in their grief.*

Writing Christian a letter helped me resolve any unfinished conversations that needed to happen. I quietly slipped this into his coffin before the final internment. My letter went something like this:

> Son,
>
> I am angry, and I am sad. Why couldn't you talk with us? Why couldn't you wait one more day? Do you not see the devastation you have brought to our family?
>
> I am sorry for my unkind words to you throughout the years. I wish I had been more patient with

you. I wish our relationship had been closer. I wish
you would walk through the door so I could tell
you how much I love you.
    Love,
    Mom

I also had him "write" back to me by dictating the
words which came into my mind as I sat with pen to paper.
His response went something like this:

   Dear Mom,
   I am so sorry for all the pain I caused you and
   Dad. I now understand how much you cared about
   me. I remember the good times when you would
   color with me as a child or cook the special food I
   liked.
   I regret the times I turned away from you when
   you were just trying to have a conversation with
   me. I wish I had tried harder in our relationship.
       Love,
       Christian

I know I can continue to write to him as well as have
him respond in this way if needed.

Another tool that has been highly effective for me is
meditation. Each morning and evening I continue to visualize Christian as part of our family circle. "Seeing" him
every day surrounded by our family reminds me we are
still together. I also have an occasional desire to physically
touch him and hug him like I used to do when he would

enter or leave the house. I visualize myself holding him, then looking into his eyes and telling him how much I love and miss him. At times this can feel very real and fulfills my need to touch and talk with him.

It's been important for our family to honor each other's stages in their grief cycle. Because both our past experiences and the level of our relationships with Christian varied, we are moving through this cycle at different speeds. I was ready to move forward fairly quickly and found healing through sharing my story. The rest of the family did not move as quickly, and I found myself feeling frustrated at times. They, in turn, felt frustrated that I so readily talked about his suicide and shared my heart with strangers.

My younger daughter, Victoria, was not prepared to talk about Christian. Even the mention of his name would drive her from the room. Knowing she would have to confront his suicide at some point in her life in order to heal, I tried to force discussion on her. This only led to her becoming angry with me. I had to stop forcing conversation with her about Christian, while still allowing myself the space to acknowledge and honor my son.

When Victoria started at the U of U that fall, she was struggling as the only child left in the house, having to pass by Christian's old room every day, and attending the University that he had loved. She was looking for greater meaning in her life and reached out to the Army recruiter she had talked with in the spring.

Earlier in the year, she had sought a position as medic, but nothing was open. A recent change in the law now allowed women to serve as combat medics. There was an opening within Stephen's former guard battalion, which she immediately took. It wasn't until the day after he swore her in that Stephen realized she was part of a combat unit rather than just a medical unit, which meant the real possibility that she would be activated. After having seen so much death and destruction from his time in the Middle East, Stephen was genuinely concerned for his daughter. Victoria started her one-weekend-a-month guard duty in the fall, with plans to leave for basic training in February 2020.

My older daughter, Skye, was a bit more vocal about her brother's death, although she too contemplated a fairly drastic life change. She was able to speak a couple of times at her Alma Mater, Westminster College, about the devastating effects of suicide and how we need to be more aware of others' struggles.

She too struggled with going to work and acting as if everything was normal. Just getting out of bed and showing up took every bit of strength she possessed. Skye expressed her regrets about her relationship with Christian, and how she'd not followed up on some promptings to be kinder to him.

Her love of the outdoors had new meaning as she began to include Christian on her hiking excursions. One day she came across a bench perched off the side of the mountain overlooking the Salt Lake Valley. She would sit for hours there, finding solace in her mental conversations with him.

Skye considered quitting her corporate job and taking a position as a wilderness guide for struggling youth. As parents, we were able to talk her through the infatuation with running away from reality, but we could tell she was grieving deeply. When she told us in the fall that she wanted to go into commercial real estate, we were a bit stunned as this was in complete opposition to her current career trajectory. We were happy she was excited about anything. We wholeheartedly supported her decision. It seemed that we were all making dramatic changes in our lives.

An example of our family's varying levels of grief was on October 21, 2019—Christian's 20th birthday. I wanted to gather as a family to remember him. No one else was willing and wanted to grieve in private. Not being able to have a formal gathering felt as if he was forgotten. I was grieving not only for the loss of my son but also the loss of our family, who intentionally spent the day apart. I needed my other children to know that if they passed on, I would not forget them either, but I didn't know how to go about it.

As Christmas approached, I wanted some way to include him without making the others uncomfortable. Skye gave us a beautiful gift in the form of a plaque that reads, "In loving Memory. This light shines as a symbol of a life and love remembered. *Christian Dean Galley.*" It has a place for a candle which we burn on those occasions we want to show his presence. It's a beautiful, unobtrusive way to honor my son's place in our lives and show he is not forgotten.

I can see all too clearly why so many marriages and families fall apart after a tragedy. We want to find an answer to something that makes no sense to us, and in doing so, we often assign blame. This blame can be directed at anyone and everyone—even if it makes no sense at all.

Some people blame themselves, another family member, or even the victim himself. Stephen wanted to blame me for not having a better relationship with Christian. I wanted to blame Stephen for not supporting me in my attempts to parent our son. I quickly understood that blaming would tear our family apart. There could be no assignment of blame—not to ourselves, another family member, or even Christian. The struggle now is to move forward without all the answers or assigning blame so that our family can stay strong and support each other.

Another important component for keeping your family together is to talk candidly. Right before the Thanksgiving holiday, at the eight-month mark, my husband and I had a very raw and difficult conversation. We'd both withdrawn and were moving away from each other as we tried to cope with our grief. He snapped at me over a frustrating task, and I broke down in tears. I realized that the hard shell I had built around my heart to protect me from my military man's sometimes harsh words had shattered upon Christian's death.

The struggle now is to move forward without all the answers or assigning blame so that our family can stay strong and support each other.

I could not continue with this pattern. If I put the shell back over my heart to protect me from Stephen's words, I would be unable to continue my work to help others. Yet now that my heart was completely open and vulnerable to any unkind word or abrasive tone, what was I to do? (As a side note here, the military way of communicating can seem overbearing and harsh to those unfamiliar with it. What sounds to most people very much like shouting is actually their way of conversing.)

I told him, "I am not willing to put the protective shell back on my heart, now that I have started feeling again. I am also not willing to continue to live with a man who spends one third of his life on the couch."

He opened his mouth as if to argue with me about my mathematical statement, but after quickly doing some calculations in his head, he realized I was correct. He was either in bed, at work, or on the couch in a semi-comatose state.

I then said, "I know the other therapist you visited didn't really help much. Why don't you reach out to my friend, Kandy Graves, who specializes in NLP (Neuro Linguistic Programming) and the Epi-Genetic Technique? She assisted me in overcoming my grief and guilt after Christian

It turned out that we were both feeling the same thing—like absolute failures in every aspect of our lives: marriage, parenting, career, financial, etc.

died, and I think she might be able to help you if you're willing to try something unorthodox."

Since the traditional therapy he'd been receiving hadn't done much to improve his mental state, he said, "I'd be willing to give it a try."

We finally allowed ourselves to be open and vulnerable with each other. It turned out that we were both feeling the same thing—like absolute failures in every aspect of our lives: marriage, parenting, career, finances, etc. Nothing we'd ever achieved felt like a success. We also admitted to having thought about running away to a shack on a deserted beach and just sitting there until our grief consumed us. We were both thinking and feeling the same thing, yet if we had not talked openly, we would not have known this.

Our conversation was the turning point in our relationship and allowed us healing from misunderstandings which had developed early in our marriage. By really looking at the ugly, we were able to uncover where the rift had started and how we could repair and move forward.

Before my son's passing, I saw my husband cry only twice, and one of those times was at his mom's funeral. He was usually very stoic, showing little emotion or weakness. When my son passed, my husband would cry for days. His grief and sadness were prolonged for months. Having him open up and be vulnerable has helped to draw us closer. I feel we need each other on an emotional level like we've never needed each other in the past. We're really all each other has at this point and need to protect our union more than ever.

I am a different person from the one who existed before Christian's suicide. The person I was before felt awkward talking with others about the death of a loved one—especially the loss of a child. Why did they bring it up so often? Why was their child's picture on their Christmas card? Could we just pretend the child didn't exist so the rest of us could stop feeling uncomfortable? I didn't understand that this person, although deceased, was still very much a part of their lives, that the child continued to exist and was often referred to in the present tense. I refer to my son in the present tense all the time. He is still very real to me. I honor his life by remembering and talking about him. I understand the awkwardness and try to help people through it by bringing up my son's death, so they know it's okay to talk about it with me.

People ask how I'm doing now that he's gone. This surprises me because he's not gone. In fact, I feel him close as he guides and supports me in my mission to share his story and help others. We are closer now than before his death. I know he is not in the same frame of mind as when he wrote his last note. He is free of the mental pain that tormented and pushed him to make short-sighted choices. I know he understands why I parented the way I did and that it was because I loved him that I cared so much. This boy named Christian, who said he didn't believe in God, had fulfilled his mission by helping me become a more Christ-like and loving person.

I've also noticed my grief has changed me on a cellular level. I am literally not the same person as before. I react differently to situations and events. Whereas in the past I was prompt with appointments and deadlines, now I see no reason to rush. "It will all work out," I tell myself. I've noticed this in my husband and daughter as well. I'm also not as aggressive. My type A is more often in the back seat with a healer personality driving the bus. Who is this person who is willing to hug strangers and take time to listen to their pain?

I look back and ask myself, what would I have done differently in raising my children? My husband is a retired Army Colonel, and we ran a tight ship at home. When I was a young parent, I thought that was the way you did things. You're the enforcer and all the kids fall in line.

So what would I change if I could go back and start over as a parent? I would focus on relationships. I would create a better environment in which my children felt they could talk to me about anything. "Mom, I got the girl down the street pregnant." Or, "Mom, I'm coming out. I'm gay." Instead of having these extremely strict rules or way of life, I would create an environment in which they felt comfortable telling me anything.

My role as a parent is to guide and support instead of dictate and enforce. I have given up the role as "Savior" for my children and it has lifted a burden from my shoulders and completely freed me from taking ownership of their decisions. I have never felt better about our relationship.

This boy named Christian, who said he didn't believe in God, had fulfilled his mission by helping me become a more Christ-like and loving person.

In the middle of February 2020, close to the 11-month mark, my youngest daughter left for basic combat training. She would be gone for six months with limited contact with the outside world. Due to the lockdowns from COVID-19, which started in March, we were unable to attend her graduation and saw her only once during her training. Her absence was also a difficult loss for us to bear during an already difficult time.

As I thought about our separation, I realized the situation with my son was very much the same. I knew where he was and a little bit about what he was doing, but I didn't have much contact. I knew that just like my daughter's return, I would someday be reunited with my son. I viewed the separation with each child in exactly the same light—just with different timelines.

Chapter 10

SUICIDE EPIDEMIC

*I think the saddest people always try their
hardest to make other people happy because they
know what it's like to feel absolutely worthless and
they don't want anyone else to feel like that.*

~ Robin Williams

Two months after Christian's death, my friend's adult daughter passed away from an unintentional overdose. Tracey and her family lived up the street and have been in the neighborhood for at least twenty years. I saw her daughter, Sheridan, struggle with the consequences of her choices through her teen and young adult years. I saw her parents struggle to guide this daughter they loved onto a path that would ensure her safety and happiness.

At 28, Sheridan and her three children lived with her parents, had been through multiple drug rehab programs, and had just completed a court-mandated 45-day abstinence from alcohol program. The very day her ankle bracelet came off, Sheridan started drinking again. She went away with friends for the weekend and came home Sunday evening drunk. Add to that a Lortab and sleeping pill and tragedy was imminent.

As Tracey helped Sheridan into her pajamas and bed, she wondered if she should take Sheridan to the ER, but this was like all the other times when Sheridan had drunk herself to sleep. In the end it all turned out the same in that Sheridan ended up sleeping off the hangover. Why would this time be any different? Yet this time the outcome would be different.

Since Sheridan's tolerance for alcohol had diminished with the 45-day hiatus, the amount she had consumed was too much for her slim body. Tracey found her unconscious and blue the next morning. She called the paramedics, but it was too late. Sheridan slipped away as she lay on the floor where they had desperately attempted to save her life. Tracey was devastated as she replayed her decision not to take Sheridan to the ER the night before.

I heard about Sheridan's passing that morning when Tracey's niece texted me, "Lark, Sheridan passed away from an unintentional overdose. I know you and Tracey are close. Would you please go over to her house to see what you can do to help her?"

Tracey and I have been good friends for a long time, but with the recent loss of my son, this was more than just a condolence visit. We looked into each other's eyes and knew we were experiencing a common pain.

As we talked about what happened, it was as if I were reliving the day Christian died, with all the comings and goings of official personnel, decisions to be made, and unanswered questions that all started with "Why?" The scab that had been slowly forming on my heart was picked off, and I was left feeling raw and numb again.

Another neighbor asked, "Was it hard for you to visit Tracey?"

I said, "Yes, but it is good for me to feel, as I have a tendency to block my feelings. Feelings—even something sad—remind me that I am human."

> *The scab that had been slowly forming on my heart was picked off, and I was left feeling raw and numb again.*

Another difficult event happened on the fourth month after my son's passing when my nephew called me. "Lark, my wife attempted suicide and is currently in lockdown at the hospital. She was on medication, but apparently the dose wasn't right, and she's been struggling."

That evening I met with my older daughter. We discussed our grief over Christian's passing and the sheer enormity the event played in our life. To learn that another family member had attempted suicide weighed heavily on our hearts. Did my niece understand how her actions would live for years as an empty hole in the hearts of her husband, sons, and extended family? This, on top of the loss of my son, was more painful than ever.

The week after my niece's attempt, I stopped by to talk with her. She had been dealing with postpartum depression for a while and had requested some medication from her OBGYN. She'd received some, but the dose wasn't high enough, so she still struggled. She didn't want to burden her husband, so she kept all this bottled up and began to think her family would be better off without her. One night when the pain became too much to bear, she took a bottle of pills in the hopes of finding relief.

We talked about her current medication, being willing to receive help from others, and talking openly with her husband. As a young mother, she was trying to live up to the perfectionist persona and feeling like she was failing. How could she let go of the desire to do it all herself? Was she willing to do less in order to continue to show up for her family? This was hard as she struggled to accept a more realistic vision of her role as wife and mother.

Since I've been willing to talk about mental illness and suicide, so many people have shared their struggles with me. While there are many factors which contribute to suicide, I have learned that those who feel a lack of connection with others or that they are a burden to their family are the most susceptible to suicidal ideation. I also believe genetics, social pressure, lack of nutrition, stress, and lower oxygen levels play a role in this nationwide epidemic.

In our virtually connected world, more people than ever feel disconnected to those around them. Relationships are one key to counteracting this trend. If we want to help those in need, I suggest we first be willing to listen for trigger words like, "I can't go on," or "Who cares if I'm dead," and "I'm a burden to my family." These are inviting statements, trying to get others to intervene. Those who end up taking their lives are in a complete state of hope-lessness. They have overcome the natural barrier to self-destruction and are in need of our love and support, not our condemnation.

As a twice survivor of suicide, I've carried a lot of grief and pain. I'm also an entrepreneur, which can add additional stress. Since my son's passing, I've found various resources to raise my resilience and aid me in my ability to cope with the pressures of life. I prefer a more natural approach to mental wellness when possible. I wish I had known about these tools prior to my son's death, which might have helped him cope with his difficulties. If you'd like to learn more about boosting resiliency, please visit my website www.LarkDeanGalley.com.

Another group who has repeatedly reached out to me is parents. They are concerned about their children and looking for ways to support them. As I mentioned earlier, when I got The Call, I thought, "I am not a doctor, therapist, or counselor. I am merely a concerned parent, but maybe that is enough."

In my research, I connected with Dr. Paul Jenkins, PhD Psychology. I loved his positive approach to dealing with hard topics. I also felt his parenting advice to be in line with what I have learned. Dr. Paul and I have collaborated to create some courses specifically around suicide prevention. He also offers some great online resources for those who struggle with their mental health. If you're interested in learning more, you can find this resource on my website as well.

Chapter 11

TRIBE OF QUEENS

The two most important days in your life are the day you are born and the day you find out why.

~ Mark Twain

As I set my New Year's resolutions on January 1, 2019, I determined to be more active and visible within my business community. For me this would entail attending at least one networking event per week. As the middle of January approached, my commitment wavered as the weekly event was going to be held in the evening with a less influential group of ladies. Not only did I not want to go out in the dark and cold, I also did not foresee much return on my efforts for the evening. Nevertheless, I had made a commitment to myself and was determined to follow through. This decision was to bless my life in a way I could not have imagined.

That evening I met a lovely lady named Keri Evans. She was an independent consultant for CAbi—a clothing line

I had loved and worn for over ten years. I could tell this networking thing was new for her as she had only recently shifted from being a full-time homemaker to finally carving out some time to do something she enjoyed. I was proud that she was stepping out of her comfort zone to develop new skills.

I like helping entrepreneurs and started questioning her about her marketing strategies and target audience. This is when I learned her husband was a famous author. She brought this up hesitantly, as she was probably used to getting bombarded with questions surrounding his career. I'm not one to pry about such things and didn't want Keri to feel like he was the reason I was taking her under my wing, so to speak, so I didn't pursue the topic. I suggested a couple of networking groups that might be a better fit for her products and later followed up to invite her to attend one of these with me in early February.

In April, the month after my son died, she was at this same networking group where I stood up to talk about his suicide and how I was speaking up to promote awareness. Keri had been following me on Facebook and knew what I'd been going through. She brought me two books that day, one of which was *The Christmas Box* written by Richard Paul Evans. The mystery of the famous author husband was finally solved.

I was familiar with the book and asked, "Did you and Richard ever lose a child? How did he come up with such a story, since it's often hard to conceive and convey such deep grief unless you've actually lived it?"

Keri told me, "No, we didn't lose a child. It was actually Richard's mom who had a stillborn daughter. The baby was taken from the room before his mom could even hold her. Richard said the story was inspiration directly from a sibling he'd known nothing about for most of his life."

Over the next several months, Keri would occasionally tell Richard about me and what I was doing to educate others on suicide prevention. During this time, I learned about an organizer he had put together. I attended one of his meetings to find out more. I liked that this planner focused on relationships over tasks because suddenly this was the most important part of life. At the meeting, I introduced myself and we chatted briefly.

Later that fall, a mutual friend, who was working with Richard to promote his organizer to businesses, approached me about working with them. I was not interested in working the corporate angle, but became excited about their work with the military and first responders. Both groups are high risk for suicide, which is where I wanted to focus my message. If there was a tool like the organizer that could help them strengthen their relationships and thereby reduce the numbers who were taking their own life, I definitely wanted to be involved.

At the end of October, I happened to be attending a meeting in Richard's building when he came in. We chatted for a few minutes, and I could sense his complete compassion for my grief. Unlike so many others who had tried to comfort me, Richard just allowed me to express my feelings and really listened. He then gave me a signed copy of his newly published book, *Noel Street*. I had felt so much love and care from both Keri and Richard throughout the year that I sent them a note expressing how truly touched I was by their kindness toward me.

Meanwhile, January 2020 rolled around. Unlike 2019, where I laid out my goals and dedicated my life to achieving them, I was having a difficult time uncovering my "why" behind all the effort in showing up. It was during a guided meditation at a business retreat that I saw my why.

As I meditated on how my message of suicide prevention might benefit others, I saw the LSU stadium filled with over 100,000 people. (I know this number because my husband is a rabid LSU football fan and has imparted many unrequested LSU tidbits throughout the years.) In my mind's eye I saw myself standing on a raised platform with each of these 100,000 people walking across the stage thanking me for helping them to choose to stay in their body. The realization that I could have such a huge impact overwhelmed me and infused my "why" to my very core.

January was also the month I dedicated myself to finishing my book. I had written some portions of it, but I was finding the emotions tied to my story very heavy and sad. I was examining my life on a deeper level than ever before and things did not always look nice down there. I was also reliving all of the grief and sorrow these events had originally created. Needless to say, I did not look forward to the time I spent writing.

I knew I needed help with the promotion of my book, as my goal was to reach as many people as possible. Who did I know who could assist me with this? You guessed it—Richard Paul Evans, who has been a #1 *New York Times* bestselling author forty times. This is why on the evening of January 22, 2020, I was praying specifically to come into closer personal contact with Richard to convince him of my mission and solicit his help.

While the interest from the military and first responders for his organizer had not panned out as we'd hoped, I was still involved in one of his Facebook groups. The morning after my prayer, Richard posted in the group that he would be holding a special Queens Imperium training for women that coming Saturday—only two days away. While I was intrigued, I also had some prior commitments and felt I could not change them, so I did not sign up. "I'll do it later," I told myself.

That evening as I was praying, God reprimanded me. "I answered your prayer and you told me no?" I then realized what I had done and promised, "I'll sign up first thing in the morning."

Unbeknownst to me, at the same time Richard was asking his assistant, Diane, "Did Lark sign up for the event?"

"No, she hasn't."

"Will you get her number for me so I can personally invite her? I don't know why, but she needs to be there." Keep in mind, we'd only had one meaningful conversation and that was about my son. Richard had no idea about my background, skills, or why I needed to attend.

Needless to say, I was at the training on Saturday. We were both amazed when we heard each other's stories about how I ended up coming. We agreed to meet the following week to discuss how Queens Imperium could bless the lives of thousands of women. When he learned about all I was currently doing, he asked, "Why would you want one more job?"

"Queens Imperium aligns with my mission to help women heal their relationships, and the mission is more important than anything else I am working on."

Queens Imperium seminars quickly morphed into the organization, Tribe of Queens. One of the goals was to support anti-human trafficking, as this tends to affect women and mothers specifically. Initially we thought this might just include writing a check to a foundation, but as we presented our goal to dedicate one million dollars to this cause, we realized how passionate the women were about stopping the trafficking. Additionally, the women let us know they wanted to be more involved with these efforts rather than simply writing a check. They wanted to actively participate in educating the public and providing aftercare to those rescued from slavery.

Suddenly, the idea for our own anti-trafficking movement was hatched with Tribe of Queens being the army behind implementing our goals. The vision caught on, and we began to grow faster than ever. The Christmas Box House, Richard's foundation for abandoned and abused children, created a division to specifically save children from trafficking. It was a natural extension of his personal mission. Before the division was even created, we had offers of donations by large corporations and private donors who also wanted to be involved.

I love that we educate the youth on how predators are targeting them. I also think it's important to help our children find their value within themselves rather than outside in someone or something. By strengthening their self-esteem, we can keep them away from both predators and feelings of hopelessness that may drive them toward suicide. While I've experienced the pain of losing a child, at least I have some closure. I cannot begin to imagine the horror of going to bed at night not knowing where my child was or what they might be experiencing.

As Richard and I have worked together to build Tribe of Queens, we have separately received, on multiple occasions, the same inspiration on how to grow the company. We excitedly share insights which the other one has already received. This validates my belief that what we are working on is bigger than either one of us.

I also realize how my background and skill set has set me up to perfectly support Tribe of Queens. I've had experience in global sales and operations working with large, multina-

While I've experienced the pain of losing a child, at least I have some closure. I cannot begin to imagine the horror of going to bed at night not knowing where my child was or what they might be experiencing.

tional corporations. I've run several of my own businesses, am an experienced speaker, and can train others on how to present. Looking back on what I would term a varied skill set, I see that God has been preparing me my entire life to fill a role that blesses the lives of so many.

I see that God has been preparing me my entire life to fill a role that blesses the lives of so many.

Tribe of Queens officially launched April 1, 2020. Despite the global pandemic, we had over 20,000 Facebook followers within our first month. Both our followers and Tribe members continue to grow. I can see that LSU stadium filling up as I share my message of value and hope to empower women in every aspect of their lives, while at the same time blessing the lives of thousands of children. All of this because I followed the prompting to attend the networking group where I met Keri the year before and thought I might help support her. God truly is in the details.

HEALING RESPONSES

My greatest joy has been the responses from those who have heard my story and gained the strength to carry on. Here are some of those messages.

Dear Lark,

Thank you so much for reaching out to me in love and kindness. The package you sent came a few weeks ago and I recently felt ready to read some of the information. It helped me to feel more peace and to understand the reactions and feelings I have had. I was also able to listen to your podcasts this week. They were so incredibly touching, and I felt even more peace as I listened to you talk about Christian. You have been blessed with a unique talent and gift to share, and I am thankful you are acting on that prompting. You have helped me in ways I cannot describe. I cannot express my gratitude enough for you. Thank you, Lark, for sharing yourself so freely and helping me to heal.

With respect and love,

– Angie

(Friend whose son died by suicide one year after Christian.)

Dear Lark,

You reached out to me at a very dark time in my life and invited me to a seminar. Before the seminar I stayed on my couch for three months not being able to move or face life. I was frozen because I was a victim of domestic violence, and I was raped. I had a hard time coming to terms with what I had been through, but that seminar was just what I needed. It gave me the strength and the courage to keep going. Your empowering story saved my life and gave me the strength to press charges so I can prevent other girls from going through what I went through. So I just wanted to say thank you for reaching out to me that day!

– Sarah W.

(Woman in her mid-20s I have known for over ten years.)

Hi Lark,

I am one of Christian's friends from high school. I just wanted to reach out and let you know that I am very thankful for your spreading Christian's story. I got in a dark place like he did a couple of months ago. But because of what he experienced and the impact of all of this, I choose to stay because I know how much pain it causes. Thank you for all you have done. Christian was a great friend and I miss him. Thank you for all you do.

– Former classmate of Christian

Lark,

A little update from me. My wife and I have been going to counseling with our son. We have really seen an adjustment in coping language and frustration levels. I haven't heard him reverting to wanting to end things for a while now. That could be from all of us getting better strategies when frustrations arise or maybe better vocabulary to use when things have happened. Either way, we still have work to do, but I feel like we are moving in a much healthier direction. Thank you for suggesting that we intervene earlier. I appreciate it.

– Al

(Someone I met at a business networking group where I shared my son's story. He was worried enough to tell me about his concerns for his 9-year-old son. I recommended some resources beyond the school counselor.)

Lark,

I wanted to tell you that my son had a nervous breakdown last week. We were so overwhelmed, sad, and worried sick. After we were able to calm and soothe him, I expressed how worried I am that he may one day make an extreme, irreversible choice. He said that after he hugged you and Stephen at Christian's funeral, and you took the time to tell him in the midst of your tragedy to make sure to speak up and reach out for help, he would never choose that route. He said that moment changed him forever. That you and Stephen changed him forever.

– A friend and concerned mother

Facebook post by Skye Galley on March 21, 2020

A year ago today, my life completely changed when I found out my younger brother passed away. Losing Christian completely destroyed my family. His fun-loving and caring nature made him the keystone, and his physical absence left a gap felt by everyone. A few months after Christian died, my health started to decline, and my anguish eventually manifested as shingles. This was a wake-up call for me, and I knew it was time to make decisions that would help relieve my suffering so I could move forward with my life.

Before Christian died, I was doing great. I had my dream job with my dream company, and everything was amazing. After he died, the domino effect altered all aspects of my life. I began questioning everything, and my old ways of being began to slough off as my priorities shifted.

Fast forward, and my life has taken a complete 180. I recently left my comfy job to pursue a newfound passion: Commercial Real Estate. My relationship with each family member individually, and as a whole, is the strongest it has ever been. I am so proud of my family for coming together and prioritizing our relationships above everything else this past year. We are making great progress as we learn to incorporate Christian into our daily lives. He has made it clear that he is, and will be, always with us.

Today I choose to remember my loved one as the physical form I knew for 19 years as well as the spiritual being who has provided me with support, love, and hope this past year.

I write this with a heavy heart and broken spirit. My sweet baby brother has passed and is no longer with us. If you knew Christian, you knew what an incredible person he was. Christian had the biggest heart and always showed acceptance, kindness, and compassion to everyone who crossed his path.

He was ingenious and inventive; we knew he was a ~~gifted child early on. Christian would spend days, weeks,~~ and even months dedicated to his projects. He constantly took things apart just to rebuild them and learn how everything worked so he could conceptualize his new theories and creations. We knew Christian's discoveries had the potential to impact the world.

When Christian wasn't engrossed in his STEM activities, he enjoyed expressing his creativity through music. You could often find him hammering out a new song he composed on the piano.

Christian always loved and appreciated the outdoors. I think he really enjoyed it because of the fun memories he made with his fellow Boy Scouts: camping, boating and more. Christian became an Eagle Scout by 14 — a difficult feat overall, but especially at such a young age. We were always so proud of him and his accomplishments. Christian was truly a unique combination of amazing qualities: gentle, empathetic, intelligent, and imaginative.

There is a quote by Ernest Shackleton written on Christian's wall in his room, "It is in our nature to explore, to reach out into the unknown. The only true failure would be not to explore at all." Christian inspired me more than he knew. I will forever hold him near in my heart, and will constantly strive to feel his spirit with me throughout my life.

Always remember to show your loved ones how much you care; you never know when you will see them next. I love you, Christian Galley, and I will always continue to love you.

Christian at the Salt Flats six months before he died.

CHRISTIAN DEAN GALLEY OBITUARY
1999 – 2019

CHRISTIAN DEAN GALLEY, our
beloved son and brother, returned
to his Heavenly home on March
21, 2019. Christian was born on
October 21, 1999 and was one of
four children.

Christian lived in South Jordan, Utah in one neighborhood
his entire life and was surrounded
by friends and neighbors who knew and loved him. He
graduated from Itineris Early College High School and
was in his sophomore year at the University of Utah in
the mechanical engineering program. Christian had a brilliant mind and could conceptualize complex tasks even as
a young child. He played the violin, piano, and guitar and
would compose his own music so no one could tell him he
was playing it wrong.

Christian was wise beyond his years, thoughtful, loving, caring, and had a wonderful sense of humor. He had a

quick wit and would often interject one-liners that would leave everyone laughing. He enjoyed robotics, the game Magic, and driving his lime green Camaro. He also loved the outdoors, was an Eagle Scout and a member of the Order of the Arrow. Life was never dull with Christian around and his desire to design and test his experiments including setting off rockets in the house, a homemade flamethrower, and explosions in the backyard.

Christian was a wonderful son, brother, and friend. He is survived by his parents, Stephen S. and Lark Dean Galley; brother, Caleb Thurman (Diana); sisters, Skye and Victoria; grandparents David and Bevonne Crookston, and many aunts, uncles, cousins, and friends. It was a privilege to have Christian in our lives and we will always love him. He can now find peace with our Savior Jesus Christ, our Heavenly Father, and other loved ones who have preceded him in death including great-grandparents Sidney C. and Beatrice Galley and Lowell and Delsa Campbell; grandparents, Sidney J. and Kathy Galley and Larry Dean.

A viewing will be held at Jenkins-Soffe South Valley, 1007 W. South Jordan Parkway, South Jordan, Utah on Friday, March 29, 2019 from 6 to 8 p.m.. The funeral service will be held on Saturday, March 30, 2019 at 11 a.m. at the Jordan River 6th Ward Chapel on 11473 S. Chapel View Dr., South Jordan, Utah with viewing from 10 to 10:45 a.m. prior to the service.

A separate service will be held at Mothe Funeral Home in Harvey, Louisiana in April. In accordance with his wishes, Christian will be laid to rest in the Galley Family tomb.

EXCERPTS FROM RICHARD IRVING'S FUNERAL TALK FOR CHRISTIAN GALLEY

I FEEL VERY HONORED TO BE ASKED by the Galleys to speak today. I have known the Galleys since they moved into the neighborhood. I guess that means that I have known Christian since he was born. I had the privilege of being Christian's friend, home teacher, and Bishop. I was able to see Christian in his element with his family, with his friends, and with his leaders.

I was Christian's home teacher throughout his teenage years. Almost every time I visited the Galleys, we would end up in the same seating arrangement. They have two couches in their Great Room that face each other. I would be on one of the couches. Lark would always join me on my side of the room. The other kids, and I will include Stephen in this definition, would all be on the other couch. Usually in a dog pile of some kind and usually with Stephen on the bottom.

Christian knew exactly what to do to get his dad's attention during our visits. He would know when to pinch, when to poke, when to squeeze and when to bounce to cause the most "gentle" irritation with Stephen—and also with Victoria.

While there was often this bantering going on in the background, Christian had the great ability to multitask. He could talk about his latest science project or his latest curiosity and still be giving his dad or his sister a wet willy.

Christian loved his family. The dog pile was consistently created each time I came, from the time Christian was 12 or 13 until after he graduated. At 18, you have to love your family to dog pile on them—and still think it was fun.

There are a couple of words I would use to describe Christian. The first one would be inquisitive. Christian was always asking questions. He was always exploring.

I know that his mom and dad on more than one occasion needed to curb his inquisitiveness, such as the time he was making a Molotov cocktail or the times of his dry ice experiments. But what I loved about his inquisitiveness was his absolute excitement about seeing something work as planned. "Did you see that?" or "That was so cool!" were simple expressions of his love of learning.

There were times when he wanted to build a solar system that was to scale and accurate. I can't remember all the details, but the dining room was full of solar system parts.

I also remember the pure excitement in his voice as he showed me one of his latest acquisitions, his throwing stars. They were so sharp and so cool. He was thoroughly enamored with how they were made and what they could do.

Christian made his own "taser." I understand that both Caleb and Skye have felt the effects of this contraption.

Perhaps others of you have also felt it. Lark and Stephen shared the video that was made as Christian first tested the taser on himself. In the camera frame is Christian holding the device. Then it shocks Christian. He is literally "thrown" out of the camera frame and you hear his reaction at being tased; however, a second or two later, his face comes back into the camera. I was amazed at what I saw. I was expecting to see anguish, pain, writhing on the floor because of the effects of the taser. But he was utterly excited and amazed that the device worked. Again, he loved seeing the results of his planning and work. He loved the adventure of learning and doing.

Another word I would use to describe Christian is respectful. Now, to be fair, some of that respect was probably learned and not natural. Lark and Stephen taught Christian how to respect women, men, leaders, and all people. Having Stephen in the military and from the South probably helped teach that respect.

Christian loved being an explorer, he loved being a youth, but he was never disrespectful. "Yes, sir," and "Yes, ma'am," were very natural for Christian.

I understand that he was able to get out of a few traffic tickets lately. His respect was probably a very large part of only getting warnings. I am sure Christian used the phrase, "Yes, officer," more than once.

Christian was an individual. He did not just go along with the crowd. I loved that individuality. Christian demonstrated this over and over throughout his youth, but one particular example was at a youth camp in Moab. At that camp we had two tents for the youth. Christian wasn't going to sleep in either of them because he brought his own self-contained sleeping bag. I think he got it from Stephen. It was a camouflage design and somehow zipped up, completely covering the person. No body part was exposed. So, the first night he got in his sleeping bag, zipped it up, and went to sleep.

The only problem was that it was right in the middle of camp. Between the tents and in the walking paths to the tents and the river. It was dark and the bag was camouflaged, so we tripped over him. But he was okay. He slept soundly in his zipped up camouflaged sleeping bag. Even when the camp was fully awake, Christian was sleeping soundly in his bag in the middle of camp.

Lark and Stephen shared with me another great example of how Christian was his own person. Last year, Christian and Stephen went to China together. One of their activities was to get a handmade suit. This took effort. They had to get measured (about fifty different ways) and then they needed to find their own material for the suit. I am sure the tailor probably had some stock material that many people would use, but Christian had to find his own material. He had to find two materials, actually. One material for the actual suit and one material for the lining.

Well, Christian and Stephen looked and looked. Christian finally found what he was searching for. As I understand it, both Stephen and the tailor tried to talk him out of the material. But he would have none of it. He knew what he wanted, and he stuck to his decision. He chose a shockingly bright blue color that looked more appropriate on a pimp than a young man. This is truly a one-of-a-kind suit that fits Christian perfectly.

Christian loved all things Harry Potter. He particularly loved a little stuffed toy that he got when he was six years old called Scabbers—a little rat.

Scabbers has quite a history in the Galley home. Christian would take Scabbers everywhere and kept it with him always. But somehow, Scabbers would get lost. The Galleys don't know how he would get lost, but he could not be found anywhere they looked. Scabbers would go missing for weeks or months, but somehow, he would always come back. He would always show up at some point.

When he did show up, he was loved and taken everywhere by Christian again. And he would get lost, again. But he would always come back.

During one of Stephens's deployments to Afghanistan with the military, Christian snuck Scabbers into Stephen's duffel bag. Not just on the top but deep inside. Stephen did not know Scabbers was there until he emptied the duffel bag on his cot in Afghanistan.

Christian gave Scabbers to Stephen because he knew that Scabbers always came back. If Stephen had Scabbers, then Stephen was coming back too. Both Stephen and Scabbers came back from that deployment.

The next time Stephen left, Christian made sure that Stephen had Scabbers. From what I understand, Scabbers has seen the world. Stephen would actually take Scabbers on missions with him, so that he would come back.

Well, now it is Christian, not Scabbers, who is gone for a time.

We have questions, we have fears, we have grief, we feel intense pain, and we feel a void or a hole in our lives. And we certainly don't have all the answers.

But let's look at what we do know:

1. We know that we do not know the whole story. I learned an important lesson in my early days as a bishop. I learned that no one knows the entire story. We see experiences and events from our own perspective. But unless we are that person, we don't know the whole story. So only Christian and our Heavenly Father know the whole story. And we must leave it at that.

2. But we do know that this earthly life is just a portion of our existence. We came from God and we will return to Him. Christian has been taken home. He has been reunited with loved ones and he has met others he did not know in this life.

3. We also know that we will continue to learn after this life. We have not yet mastered chemistry or physics. Yet we need this knowledge to be exalted. Christian was far more advanced in these areas than most of us. But there are other things he may be learning. He is still being taught. And, knowing Christian, he is still learning…. And understanding. Perhaps he is being taught that faith and science do coexist in harmony with each other.

4. We know that we are grieving, and we know that grief is part of our experience when we lose a loved one. The grieving process can last for a long time and it is not all going to be better tomorrow. That is okay. We have to grieve.

5. But, we know that the Atonement of Jesus Christ is for all men. Christ has felt Christian's pain, whatever it was, and he has felt Lark's, Stephen's, Skye's, Victoria's, Caleb's, and every other person's pain so that he can succor us all. Succor means to assist and support in times of hardship and distress. We know that this is one of those times.

Stephen, Lark, kids . . . the Savior knows your grief. He knows your heartache. He knows your sorrow. Because of His Atonement, you (and we) can find peace.

Because of the plan of salvation, the Savior's atonement and His resurrection, Christian, like Scabbers, will come back. We will be able to be reunited with him again. The joy you will feel when the reunion takes place will far exceed the joy anyone felt when Scabbers or Stephen first came back. How great will be your joy when you see and understand what this time away, what the atonement and what the resurrection have done for Christian.

EXCERPTS FROM FUNERAL TALK
BY MARC HALE

I'M HONORED TO BE HERE TODAY. I've been blessed to be able to work with the young men in several different capacities over the past fifteen years which has brought me a lot of joy. Since I heard that Christian had passed, I've spent a lot of time reliving those experiences.

I've been on a fair number of campouts and activities with Christian and there was always one common thread: Christian always came prepared for the zombie apocalypse. Although he was much more likely to encounter a squirrel than a zombie. Even in the worst-case scenario, I'm not sure how he expected to stop a charging bear with a throwing star, but I'm sure he would have figured out a way to do it.

I remember a boys' camp where the plan was to hike up to Timpanogos. It was an overnighter, so the boys had to pack in food and sleeping gear. By the time we were a couple hours into the hike, Christian and Jansen were exhausted because of the weight of their packs. After an inspection, the leaders found machetes, numb chucks, and several knives. You know, just the essentials!

My favorite experience happened, I think it was in Lake Powell, when Christian had gathered the boys (away from all the leaders of course) and was convincing them that it was a good idea to let him try out his homemade taser on them. He was surprised and bewildered when I told him I didn't think that it was a good idea. He looked at me like "was that wrong?" I'll miss that about Christian.

We have been sent here to earth to have an experience. I think one of our greatest blessings is to be able to know that this life is not the entire story. In fact, once we pass on from this life, we'll find that our time here on earth was just a brief moment. I believe that Christian has a spirit that has left his body and entered the spirit world and that he's not that far from us.

Just a couple of days ago, we went to visit Lark, Stephen, and Victoria in their home. It was amazing to be able to talk to them about some of our memories of Christian. I was struck with a range of emotions that I'm sure each of us feel at this time. We laughed as we talked about some of the crazy things Christian would do. I also felt sad knowing that those experiences have been cut short. But overall, there was this intense feeling of peace and love. I could feel the Holy Ghost, and just as clearly, I could feel Christian, he was there and participating. I'm sure that he's also here with us today.

One time we went to a scout camp in the Uintahs with Christian. When we got there, he asked me if we had any rope. I'd had enough experience with Christian to be a little nervous anytime he had a project in mind. Besides, he needed to get to class. I told him to get to class and I left with several of the boys to get them to their merit badge classes. Well, Christian never went to class, by the time we got back, he had found his rope and had carefully weaved it into a hammock, and was taking a nap. Never mind that his dad had left Ken Woolley and me with strict instructions that Christian was to be in class.

I'll be honest that I was a little nervous when Stephen got there, that we were in trouble for not making Christian go to class. But I'll never forget how excited Christian was to show his dad the hammock and how Stephen was so impressed with it that he forgot that we hadn't done our job. I owe you one for that, Christian.

I would like to conclude with a word of advice to the heavenly individual who is checking Christian in. If you haven't found his knife yet, keep looking. It's hidden somewhere on his person.

Epilogue

SHORTLY BEFORE MY BOOK WAS OFFICIALLY RELEASED, I received an email from a friend of Christian's. She had an advance reader copy and sent me the following message. It allowed me some insight into what Christian was feeling as well as his desire to improve our relationship. Her dreams also confirmed what I had been feeling—that Christian is nearby and glad that I am sharing his story.

Dear Lark,

I was very close friends with Christian through high school. We talked a lot about our home life and future. I have wanted to reach out but didn't know how or when. After reading your book, it seemed like the universe was pushing me to contact you.

Christian and I didn't become close friends until the middle of our junior year. I had a really rough time that year and everyone could see it, but no one understood or knew how to help. Christian forced me to laugh and come out of my shell. I think he saw himself in me. After a few weeks of just seeing each other at school and texting, we became great friends and were able to talk on a significantly deeper level.

During this time, he started to tell me about the tension in his relationship with you and how he wished he knew how to fix it. He talked about how he loved you but felt like he was making all the wrong steps. It was similar to my relationship with my father. We would trade advice on things we found that worked in our own relationship with our parents.

Even though he told me he got along with his dad better than you, he would always talk about wanting a better relationship with you. Reading about the efforts you made to try and improve your relationship with Christian made me realize how much you guys wanted the same thing. I'm not going to lie; it made me cry knowing how hard you were both trying even though it was such a difficult task.

I remember so many times Christian said he thought his relationship with you was improving a little. These were the times he looked happier than I had ever seen him. I think he always wanted to be closer despite what it seemed like. It was just difficult to communicate effectively. We were teenagers, so we didn't always know the best ways.

After graduation, we drifted apart. I remember on the night of March 20th I had the weirdest feeling that I needed to call him. I regret not calling even though I know I couldn't have done anything. We had sent a text or two that day, so I chalked my feeling up to missing him. At noon the next day, I saw I had about ten missed calls from a mutual friend. I brushed it off because she didn't leave a message or text. Then I got another call from a mutual friend who told me Christian was dead. I couldn't breathe.

I just sank against a wall. I know I called my mom and went over to her house, but I couldn't tell you how I did it.

One of the things I will most regret was not reaching out to you before he died. Christian told me once or twice how he would kill himself. I knew his having a plan was concerning, but he wasn't doing any of the suicide signs like giving things away or exhibiting erratic behavior. He also told me, "I would never be able to kill myself. It's a coward's exit, and I couldn't do that to my friends and family." I wish I had said something to you.

I have also had a few dreams where he is there. They are too realistic for me to believe they are false. One thing that sticks out specifically is he always mentions how proud he is about what you're doing. In the most recent dream, a few weeks ago, he said to tell you, "I know my mom won't believe it, but tell her anytime she thinks I'm there, I am and to not doubt it. It's me, and I'm with her."

Thank you so much for everything you've been doing. I've listened to most of the podcasts you've done especially when there are bad grief days. They have helped so much. I was apprehensive when I first heard you were writing a book, but it is beyond perfect. I know I will come back to it again and again; it is so well done. Christian set a legacy that you are carrying out and I am so happy to witness it. He was always larger than life and knowing you are helping him be larger in death is amazing. Thank you for everything you are doing.

Sincerely,
Lexy B.

Acknowledgments

I WANT TO EXPRESS MY APPRECIATION to my extended family, friends, and neighbors who reached out in our time of need. They truly have been the personification of bearing one another's burdens, and we would not have made it without them.

I would also like to thank Richard Paul Evans, for taking time out of his busy schedule to write the Foreword for this book. His kindness, influence, and mentorship have guided me in this process and helped me find healing as I've shared my story.

A special thank you to Sterling R. Walker, Evelyn E. Jeffries, Francine Platt, and Karen Christoffersen for their help in editing and laying out this book for publication. It would have been a quite different book without their insight and knowledge.

I want to acknowledge the beautiful photography of my friend, Stephanie Ann Bagley, who was instrumental in taking so many of the professional photographs you see throughout my book.

I also want to express my love to my mother, who instilled in me the faith and strength to go on when it felt easier to stop.

And finally, to my Heavenly Father and Savior, Jesus Christ. May I, in some small way, be an instrument in Thy hands to further Thy message of love and hope.

About the Author

LARK DEAN GALLEY IS THE MOTHER of Christian Dean Galley, who passed away by suicide in March 2019. Sharing his story brings her joy and has allowed her to heal their relationship.

Lark is married to Stephen S. Galley, LTC(R) and is the mother to three other children and grandmother to four. She lives with her husband, youngest daughter, and rescued cat, Mudd, in the Salt Lake Valley.

After years of pushing herself, Lark has finally learned the power of slowing down and connecting. She enjoys spending time with her family, being in nature, and riding her AirChair which some say she is too old to do.

Contact

If you would like to reach out to Lark, here is how to do it.

Lark@LarkDeanGalley.com

www.LarkDeanGalley.com

Purchase copies of *Learning to Breathe Again* at Amazon.com.
If you would like to order 50+ copies,
please reach out to Lark for a volume discount.

Regardless of where you purchase the book, I encourage you to leave a review at www.Goodreads.com. Your comments could touch someone who needs to hear your experience.

Made in USA - North Chelmsford, MA
1183973_9781606452622
01.31 2022 1647